# CONTENTS

# Introduction

**The Cannabis Issue** is the one hundred and twenty-eighth volume in the **Issues** series. The aim of this series is to offer up-to-date information about important issues in our world.

**The Cannabis Issue** looks at issues relating to cannabis use, and at cannabis' status within the law.

The information comes from a wide variety of sources and includes:
Government reports and statistics
Newspaper reports and features
Magazine articles and surveys
Website material
Literature from lobby groups
and charitable organisations.

It is hoped that, as you read about the many aspects of the issues explored in this book, you will critically evaluate the information presented. It is important that you decide whether you are being presented with facts or opinions. Does the writer give a biased or an unbiased report? If an opinion is being expressed, do you agree with the writer?

**The Cannabis Issue** offers a useful starting-point for those who need convenient access to information about the many issues involved. However, it is only a starting-point. Following each article is a URL to the relevant organisation's website, which you may wish to visit for further information.

\* \* \* \* \*

SY 0118493 8

# The Cannabis Issue

## ISSUES

## Volume 128

### Series Editor

### Lisa Firth

### Independence

Educational Publishers
Cambridge

First published by Independence
PO Box 295
Cambridge CB1 3XP
England

© Independence 2007

**Copyright**
This book is sold subject to the condition that it shall not,
by way of trade or otherwise, be lent, resold, hired out or otherwise
circulated in any form of binding or cover other than that in which it
is published without the publisher's prior consent.

**Photocopy licence**
The material in this book is protected by copyright. However, the
purchaser is free to make multiple copies of particular articles for instructional
purposes for immediate use within the purchasing institution.
Making copies of the entire book is not permitted.

**British Library Cataloguing in Publication Data**
The Cannabis Issue – (Issues Series)
I. Firth, Lisa II. Series
362.2'95

ISBN 978 1 86168 374 8

**Printed in Great Britain**
MWL Print Group Ltd

**Cover**
The illustration on the front cover is by
Don Hatcher.

# Cannabis

## Information from FRANK

Cannabis is the most widely used illegal drug in Britain. Made from parts of the cannabis plant, it's a naturally occurring drug. It is a mild sedative (often causing a chilled out feeling or actual sleepiness) and it's also a mild hallucinogen (meaning you may experience a state where you see objects and reality in a distorted way and may even hallucinate). The main active compound in cannabis is tetrahydrocannabinol (THC).

---

**There is some psychological dependence with cannabis (where there is a desire to keep taking the drug even in spite of possible harms) and this occurs in about 10% of users**

---

Slang: Bhang, black, blast, blow, blunts, Bob Hope, bush, dope, draw, ganja, grass, hash, hashish, hemp, herb, marijuana, pot, puff, Northern Lights, resin, sensi, sinsemilla, shit, skunk, smoke, soap, spliff, wacky backy, weed, zero. Some names are based on where it comes from... Afghan, homegrown, Moroccan etc.

### The effects

⇨ Some people may feel chilled out, relaxed and happy, while others have one puff and feel sick.
⇨ Others get the giggles and may become talkative.
⇨ Hunger pangs are common and are known as 'getting the munchies'.
⇨ Users may become more aware of their senses or get a feeling of

**FRANK**
0800 77 66 00 talktofrank.com
Friendly, confidential drugs advice

slowing of time, which are due to its hallucinogenic effects.
⇨ Clearly a stronger 'joint' (e.g. skunk or sinsemilla) may have more powerful effects, but users may moderate this by inhaling and using less.

### Chances of getting hooked

There is some psychological dependence with cannabis (where there is a desire to keep taking the drug even in spite of possible harms) and this occurs in about 10% of users. There are no physical withdrawal symptoms from cannabis use.

If you've only been using for a short while there should be no problem stopping but with continued regular use of cannabis, this can become more difficult. You're also at risk of getting addicted to nicotine if you roll your spliffs with tobacco.

### The law

⇨ Cannabis is illegal; it's a Class C drug.
⇨ If you're caught with cannabis: The police will always take action. What happens depends on the circumstances.

*Possession*

⇨ If you're caught with even a small amount of cannabis on you, you can be arrested. What the police will do depends on the circumstances and how old you are.
⇨ Usually, you'll get a warning and the police will confiscate the drug and if you're under 18, your parent or guardian will also be contacted.
⇨ The police are more likely to arrest you if: You are blatantly smoking in public or have been caught with cannabis before.
⇨ If you continue to break the law, you can end up with a criminal record which could affect your chances of getting a job. It could also affect whether you can go on holiday to some countries.
⇨ The maximum penalty for possession is two years in prison plus an unlimited fine.

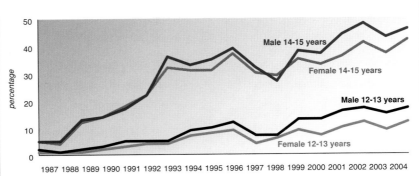

## Young people offered cannabis

Have been offered cannabis, 1987-2004. Data from the Health Related Behaviour Questionnaire from a sample of 448,124 young people between the ages of 10-15.

Male 14-15 years
Female 14-15 years
Male 12-13 years
Female 12-13 years

*Source:* Trends: Young People and Cannabis, 1987-2005, *published by the Schools Health Education Unit. Visit www.sheu.org.uk*

## Supply
⇨ Dealing is a very serious offence.
⇨ In the eyes of the law, this includes giving drugs to friends.
⇨ People who grow cannabis in their homes or carry large amounts on them also risk being charged with intent to supply.
⇨ The maximum penalty for supply is 14 years in prison plus an unlimited fine.

---

**Some people think cannabis is harmless just because it's a plant – but it isn't harmless. Cannabis, like tobacco, has lots of chemical 'nasties'**

---

*Did you know?*
⇨ Drug driving is as illegal as drink driving. You could go to prison, get a heavy fine or be disqualified.
⇨ Allowing people to take cannabis in your house or any other premises is illegal. If the police catch someone smoking cannabis in a club they can prosecute the landlord, club owner or person holding the party.
⇨ Using cannabis to relieve pain is also an offence. Possession is illegal whatever you're using it for.

### Appearance and use
Cannabis comes in different forms.

Hash is a blacky-brown lump made from the resin of the plant, and is the commonest form of cannabis in the UK. It's quite often squidgy.

Grass or weed (traditional herbal cannabis), is made from the dried leaves of the plant and looks like tightly packed dried herbs. Less common is cannabis oil, which is dark and sticky and comes in a small jar.

Recently, there have been various forms of herbal or grass-type cannabis that are generally found to be stronger than ordinary 'weed', containing on average 2-3 times the amount of the active compound, THC. These include 'sinsemilla' (a bud grown in the absence of male plants and which has no seeds), 'homegrown', 'skunk' (which has a particularly strong smell) and 'netherweed'.

These are forms of herbal cannabis often grown from selected seeds by intensive indoor methods (e.g. using hydroponic methods, artificial lighting etc.) to optimise their potency.

Most people mix cannabis with tobacco and smoke it as a spliff or a joint. Some people put it in a pipe. And others make tea with it or stick it in food like cakes or 'cannabis cookies'.

### Cost
Price varies widely around the country. Grass is usually more expensive than resin (hash), with stronger forms tending to be more expensive (e.g. 'skunk' at £200 per ounce).

### Purity
Some unsuspecting people have been known to buy blocks of mud, stock cubes and garden herbs from people pretending to be dealers.

The most impure cannabis is called 'soap bar'. It's contaminated with all sorts of things. This makes it cheaper but it's often harder to get very stoned.

It's not actually possible to tell whether a particular sample of 'skunk' or 'homegrown' or 'sinsemilla' will have a higher potency than an equal amount of 'imported herbal cannabis' – because the actual potencies of different products overlap substantially.

The potency of herbal cannabis decreases over time in storage and is affected by what parts of the plant have been included in the product. Hence, a user has little guarantee about the 'intensity of the high'. Also, it has been found the intensity of the smell of skunk appears to be no guide to the actual strength either.

### The risks
⇨ Even hardcore smokers can become anxious, panicky and suspicious.
⇨ It affects your coordination, which is one of the reasons why drug driving is just as illegal as drink driving.
⇨ Some people think cannabis is harmless just because it's a plant – but it isn't harmless. Cannabis, like tobacco, has lots of chemical 'nasties', which can cause lung disease and cancer with long-term or heavy use, especially as it is often mixed with tobacco. It can also make asthma worse.
⇨ Cannabis is risky for anyone with a heart problem as it increases the heart rate and can affect blood pressure.

⇨ There's also increasing evidence of a link between cannabis and mental health problems such as schizophrenia. If you've a history of mental health problems, depression or are experiencing paranoia, then taking this drug is not a good idea.
⇨ Frequent use of cannabis can cut a man's sperm count and suppress ovulation in women. If you're pregnant, smoking cannabis may harm the baby.
⇨ Regular, heavy use makes it difficult to learn and concentrate. Some people begin to feel tired all the time and can't seem to get motivated.
⇨ Some users may want to buy stronger herbal cannabis to get 'a bigger high' but unpleasant reactions can be more powerful when you use stronger strains, and stronger varieties may lead in time to more severe dependence or more severe mental health effects.

⇨ The above information is reprinted with kind permission from FRANK. Visit www.talktofrank.com for more information.

© FRANK

# Cannabis – in depth

## Dope, marijuana, weed, hash, skunk, grass, herb

### What is it?

Cannabis is one of the world's most commonly used leisure drugs. It is estimated that at least one person in ten in the UK has used it.

Cannabis comes from the same plant as hemp. This plant has many uses in addition to the use of cannabis as a psychoactive (or mind-altering) substance, including the manufacture of clothing, paper, plastics, building materials, food, beverages, cosmetics, methanol fuel, cleaning and paint products. Cannabis plants grow in a variety of climates and can reach up to 15 feet in height. Their leaves are made up of four to eight smaller, lance-shaped leaves with saw-toothed edges.

Although there is much debate about their origins, it is generally accepted that there are three subspecies of the cannabis *genus*. These are *Sativa* (the most prominent), *Indica* and the less favoured *Ruderalis*. Many growers cross breed these strains to produce cannabis of varying qualities.

When it is prepared for use as a psychoactive substance, cannabis comes in three main forms: cannabis resin (or hashish), herbal cannabis (or marijuana) and cannabis oil. When smoked, cannabis has a sweet,

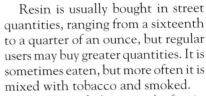

herbal smell. Stronger smelling, high strength marijuana, known as 'skunk', has become increasingly popular in recent years.

Despite an increased political interest in cannabis and the re-classification of the drug, our understanding of how cannabis works on the brain is still less than complete. We know that it contains hundreds of different chemicals, a small proportion of which are psychoactive. The most significant of these is a chemical called *delta-9 tetrahydrocannabinol* (THC). Cannabis activates cannabinoid receptors in the brain to produce a range of effects. The strength or purity of the drug is measured according to the amount of THC it contains, calculated by weight.

### Cannabis resin (Hashish)

Cannabis resin is a brown substance which is scraped from the surface of the leaves, growing buds and flowers of the plant. The resin is then sieved and pressed into a solid lump.

Resin is usually bought in street quantities, ranging from a sixteenth to a quarter of an ounce, but regular users may buy greater quantities. It is sometimes eaten, but more often it is mixed with tobacco and smoked.

The strength (or purity) of resin varies enormously. More than two-thirds of cannabis sold in the UK comes from Morocco, which exports much of the world's poorest quality cannabis. Moroccan cannabis resin generally varies from a low 2% purity to a moderate 8%. Higher quality hashish is available from Morocco and the Middle East, with purity levels of up to 20%. As with most products, the better the quality, the higher the price.

### Herbal cannabis (Marijuana)

The reduced availability of good quality cannabis resin and the wider availability of good quality herbal cannabis has caused a growing trend to use this form of the drug.

Herbal cannabis is produced by drying the leaves and flowering buds of the cannabis plant. It looks like dried herbs and may be mixed with stems and seeds. It is smoked, usually with tobacco, in a 'spliff' or 'joint', or in a range of purpose-made or home built pipes.

Herbal cannabis is imported from the Caribbean, Holland, Africa and South America, with purity ranging from around 8% to 17%.

### Skunk

Skunk is a more potent variant of herbal cannabis, both in its mind-altering effects and its aroma (hence the name). It emerged from Holland in the late 1980s, and impressed devotees so rapidly that all high strength varieties have today adopted that generic description. Often the labelling of cannabis as 'skunk' has no bearing on its actual content. Many varieties sold as skunk are no more than mass-produced standard cannabis variants.

Skunk is produced by using a variety of cultivation techniques to produce specific, desired effects. These

techniques include organic methods, hydroponic culture (using controlled heat, lighting and liquid feed) and specialised plant training techniques. Plant characteristics can be altered by cross pollination, varying nurture and storage environments, light and water management and harvesting stages. The drug is then prepared for use by drying the unfertilised female, flowering buds of a mature cannabis plant.

Before skunk became widely available, a seedless cannabis variety, called sinsemilla, was common. This variety was similar in strength to skunk but naturally occurring, rather than artificially modified.

---

**It appears indisputable that cannabis does have a detrimental effect on the mental health of a minority of individuals**

---

It is worth noting that very high quality hashish may contain more THC than an equivalent amount of skunk.

### Home-grown cannabis

The increased popularity of herbal cannabis has coincided with a trend towards growing cannabis at home. This carries serious legal risks. However, it can promote better knowledge of the effects of the drug among users, and can allow quality and quantity control, thereby reducing the risks associated with use. It can also allow growers to test their product and to try and produce qualities other than high strength, and the risks that brings with it. That said, the THC levels in home-produced herbal cannabis have been known to attain 27% under special conditions. Many of the growing techniques are common with the preparation of skunk (see above).

### Cannabis oil

Cannabis oil is a treacle-like liquid, refined from cannabis resin or, less frequently, from the plant itself. The oil is prepared by solvent extraction of the plant material or resin, and yields a particularly powerful form of the drug. It is smoked with ordinary tobacco, either by mixing it with the tobacco or by smearing it on cigarette paper which is then used to roll up tobacco.

## Desired effects of cannabis

*'The brain and organism on which hashish operates will produce only the normal phenomena peculiar to that individual – increased admittedly, in number and force, but always faithful to their origin. A man will never escape from his destined physical and moral temperament: hashish will be a mirror of his impressions and private thoughts – a magnifying mirror it is true, but only a mirror.' Charles Baudelaire (1821-1867)*

### Recreational effects

The effects of the drug depend upon the type of cannabis used, as well as your mood, your surroundings and the amount taken. The drug may bring on feelings of contentment, relaxation and happiness. Heightened sensory perception may be experienced, particularly in relation to colours and sound. Many people also attest to the aphrodisiac effects of cannabis.

### Medicinal applications

Cannabis is considered by many to have beneficial medicinal applications as an appetite stimulant, muscle relaxant, anxiety-reducing drug and analgesic. There is a considerable amount of research being done in the UK at the moment, looking at the possible benefits of cannabis for the treatment of muscular and somatic pain, and the symptoms of multiple sclerosis (MS) and wasting diseases, amongst others.

There is a strong research base to support the use of cannabis to control nausea. More recent research supports the beneficial effects of cannabis and THC-based medications in the treatment of symptoms arising from conditions such as MS and AIDS; for example, as an appetite stimulant to combat physical wasting.

Most medicinal cannabis is low in THC content. It usually comes in a capsule or as a sub-lingual spray. Cannabis is not generally available in medicinal form in the UK, although trials are being carried out into its possible medicinal uses. There is continuing debate as to whether the medicinal benefits of cannabis outweigh any harmful side effects (see below). The Court of Appeal decided in May 2005 that it was not a defence against cannabis charges to argue that it was required for medical purposes.

## Harmful effects of cannabis

The reclassification of cannabis should not be viewed as a signal that cannabis is a safe drug. Its continuing inclusion in the list of controlled substances reflects the consensus that this is not the case.

The risks associated with cannabis use are increased by lack of knowledge about the strength of the cannabis being used, as well as the risk of adulterants being present. The increased availability of high strength cannabis increases some of these risks, including adverse effects on mental health. It is, however, impossible to take a lethal dose of cannabis.

Some relatively minor side effects include tiredness, reddening of the eyes, increased appetite (due to reduced blood sugar levels) and a dry mouth. More serious side effects include an increase in your pulse rate and a drop in blood pressure. Other harmful effects of cannabis are considered below.

### Interaction with medication

As with all drugs, users should be aware of any potential harmful interaction with prescribed or 'over the counter' (OTC) medication. Please contact your doctor or Release for specific advice.

### Effects on concentration, co-ordination and reflexes

Concentration levels, coordination and reflexes can be affected while under the influence of cannabis, as well as the perception of distance and speed. It is therefore dangerous to drive or operate machinery when using cannabis.

### Effects on short-term memory

The *hippocampus*, an area of the brain implicated in the processing and retention of new memories, is particularly rich in cannabinoid receptors. Recent research, based on experiments using rats and primates, suggests that previously learned tasks are unaffected by cannabis use, but that short-term memory and the ability to learn may be affected when under the influence of cannabis.

These experimental findings are corroborated by the anecdotal reports of cannabis users. For example, of the man who composed great guitar riffs in his head when smoking, but had forgotten them by the time he got home to a guitar.

This research causes concern about young people using cannabis at a time in their lives when learning is of key importance. However, the research has not been conclusively supported by studies using human subjects.

### Effects of smoking

Smoking is by far the most common method of taking cannabis. Like tobacco, cannabis smoke contains toxins that are known to be hazardous to the respiratory system. These toxins are essentially a byproduct of combustion, separate from the THC and other pharmaceutically active components of cannabis. Although there is no proof that smoking cannabis (without tobacco) causes cancer, heavy users have been shown to be more at risk of bronchitis and respiratory infections.

One alternative to smoking is to eat cannabis, either on its own or in a variety of forms ranging from tea to cakes. However, the effects of eating cannabis can be far less predictable, partly because people often do not measure the quantity as carefully, or may not know how much of the drug is being consumed. The effects of ingesting cannabis can also vary widely between individuals.

Other alternatives to smoking cannabis with tobacco include using pipes, of varying sophistication, or vaporisers. Vaporisation is a technique used to avoid inhaling the irritating respiratory toxins in cannabis smoke. Further research is required into the carcinogenic effects of smoking cannabis, and safer ways of using the drug.

### Effects on mental health

Most people who use cannabis will never experience mental health problems as a result. However, it appears indisputable that cannabis does have a detrimental effect on the mental health of a minority of individuals. The risks seem to be highest for young people, those who use cannabis heavily and those who suffer from, or have a vulnerability to, mental illness.

Few well-controlled studies have been carried out, and those that have still fail to replicate findings. In view of the widespread use of cannabis, and the implications these findings have on general public health, better evidence is clearly needed.

The Advisory Council on the Misuse of Drugs (ACMD) published a report in March 2002 which stated that there was no conclusive evidence to suggest a causal link between smoking cannabis and the development of mental health problems.

Several subsequent reports have disputed this. One recent study (Fergusson, Horwood & Ridder, 2005) concluded that regular cannabis use may increase the risk of psychosis. Another study (Van Os et al., 2005) concluded that cannabis use moderately increases the risk of psychotic disorders, but that the risk was considerably greater for those with an established vulnerability to psychosis.

Other studies have reached seemingly contradictory conclusions. For instance, a 2004 report (MacLeod et al.) reviewed a number of longitudinal studies and concluded that the available evidence did not strongly support an important causal relation between cannabis use by young people and psychosocial harm. However, they could not exclude this possibility.

There are significant limitations on the research methods used in most of these studies. Most are reliant on self-reports of cannabis use, which often results in under-reporting, especially if the information is not collected anonymously. In addition, the diagnosis of mental health disorders is notoriously difficult. For example, heavy cannabis use can produce temporary psychotic states which may be diagnosed as schizophrenia. However, these temporary psychoses have not been proven to be a cause of psychiatric disorders.

There is often a time lapse between cannabis use and the onset of psychiatric disorders. Furthermore, other factors such as general health, family and social relations, education and employment are difficult to exclude. Genetic predisposition is another complicating factor. It is also difficult to isolate the effects of cannabis in circumstances where it is often used in conjunction with other substances.

The wider availability of higher strength cannabis, and concerns about its implications for mental health, have led to further debate about its legal classification.

⇨ Release is the national centre of expertise on drugs, the law and human rights, providing free legal services to the socially excluded. Release relies on charitable donations to continue its work – please go to www.release. org.uk if you would like to make a contribution.

© Release

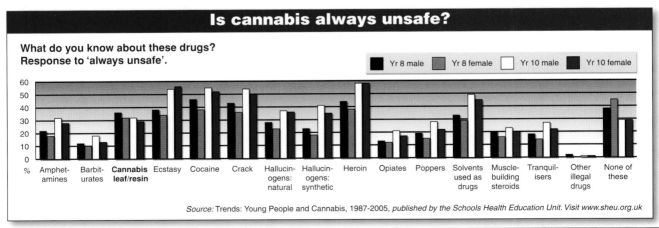

**Is cannabis always unsafe?**

**What do you know about these drugs? Response to 'always unsafe'.**

Legend: ■ Yr 8 male  ▨ Yr 8 female  ☐ Yr 10 male  ■ Yr 10 female

Categories (%): Amphetamines, Barbiturates, **Cannabis leaf/resin**, Ecstasy, Cocaine, Crack, Hallucinogens: natural, Hallucinogens: synthetic, Heroin, Opiates, Poppers, Solvents used as drugs, Muscle-building steroids, Tranquilisers, Other illegal drugs, None of these

*Source:* Trends: Young People and Cannabis, 1987-2005, *published by the Schools Health Education Unit. Visit www.sheu.org.uk*

# Cannabis facts

**Bhang, black, blast, blow, blunts, Bob Hope, bush, dope, draw, ganga, grass, hash, hashish, hemp, herb, marijuana, pot, puff, Northern Lights, resin, sensi, sensemilla, skunk, smoke, spliff, wacky backy, weed, zero etc.**

Cannabis is a plant found wild in most parts of the world and is easily cultivated in temperate climates such as the UK's. Some names are based on country of origin such as Afghan, Colombian, homegrown, Lebanese, Moroccan, Pakistani etc. Cannabis comes from *Cannabis sativa*, a bushy plant that grows in many parts of the world and is also cultivated in the UK. The main active ingredients in cannabis are the tetrahydrocannabinols (THC). These are the chemicals that cause the effect on the brain.

Different forms of cannabis come from different parts of the plant and have different strengths. 'Hashish' or 'hash' is the commonest form found in the UK. It is resin scraped or rubbed from the dried plant and then pressed into brown/black blocks. It is mostly imported from Morocco, Pakistan, the Lebanon and Afghanistan (or Nepal). Herbal cannabis is made from the chopped, dried leaves of the plant. It is also known as 'grass', 'bush' and 'ganga' and in America as 'marijuana' and is imported from Africa, South America, Thailand and the West Indies. Some is 'homegrown' and cultivated in this country, sometimes on a large scale to sell but usually by individuals in their homes or greenhouses for their own use.

Herbal cannabis is usually not as strong as the resin form. However, some particularly strong herbal forms such as 'sinsemilla' and 'skunk' have recently been cultivated in Holland and this country.

Cannabis oil is the least common form of cannabis found in the UK. It is made by percolating a solvent through the resin.

In the UK cannabis is usually smoked rolled into a cigarette or 'joint', often with tobacco. The herbal form is sometimes made into a cigarette without using tobacco. Cannabis is also sometimes smoked

in a pipe, brewed into a tea or cooked into cakes.

Hemp is the fibre of the cannabis plant. For centuries to the present day it has been used to make all sorts of products including rope, mats, clothing, cooking oil, fuel, fishing nets, cosmetics, herbal remedies, paints and varnishes.

## Potency

Recently many have believed that cannabis is becoming stronger. The EMCDDA released a European review of cannabis potency in June 2004. The study revealed that when the overall potency of cannabis products on the market is calculated, there is no evidence of a significant increase in potency. This is because, in most EU countries, imported cannabis dominates the market and this has remained stable over many years. A report of the study can be found on EMCDDA Drugnet (July-Sept 2004) http://www.emcdda. eu.int/?nNodeID=411

The full report can be found at http://www.emcdda.eu.int/index. cfm?fuseaction=public.Content&n NodeID=429&sLanguageISO=EN

## Prevalence

Cannabis is the most widely used illegal drug in the UK and easily the illegal drug most likely to have been tried by young people. *Drug Misuse Declared: Findings from the 2004/05 British Crime Survey* http:// www.homeoffice.gov.uk/rds/pdfs05/ hosb1605.pdf (PDF) show that 9.7% of 16- to 59-year-olds reported having used cannabis in the last year. In total over 9 million people in the 16 to 59 age group have used it at least once

with just over 3 million having used it in the last year.

Figures from the Department of Health survey *Smoking, Drinking and Drug Use among young people in England 2004* http://www.dh.gov.uk/ assetRoot/04/11/81/54/04118154. pdf (PDF) show that cannabis use by 11- to 15-year-olds decreased from 13% in 2003 to 11% in 2004. Prevalence of taking cannabis was slightly higher among boys (12%) than girls (10%)and increased with age: 1% of 11-year-olds had taken the drug in the last year compared with 26% of 15-year-olds.

There has been much debate about the legal status of cannabis. In general, government-commissioned reports in the English-speaking world have recommended relaxation of the existing cannabis laws. These views are shared by a number of academics, politicians and senior law enforcers.

During the 1990s, on the back of renewed interest about drug use among young people, the cannabis reform lobby took various guises ranging from the Green Party and the UK Cannabis Alliance to supportive editorials in the broadsheets and in particular the pro-reform campaign of the *Independent on Sunday*. The Liberal Democrats have supported legal changes and lobbied for a Royal Commission to explore the issues.

## Price and product

Bought on the streets, resin costs around £80 per ounce or £16 for an eighth of an ounce. Herbal cannabis costs anything from £70 per ounce to £120 for strong strains such as skunk. (source – *Independent Drug Monitoring Unit Drug Prices*). Heavy and regular cannabis users might use an eighth of an ounce per day. Many people only smoke occasionally.

Recently, stronger types of herbal cannabis have become available with names like northern lights and super skunk. They are grown from specially cultivated seeds, often imported from Holland.

The effects of these strains are more pronounced and can cause hallucinogenic effects. Some people may find them too strong and the experience of smoking them very disturbing, while others may enjoy the greater effects. Increasing amounts of these strains are being homegrown for private use or sold on the cash market and among friends.

## The public and political debate

The trend in UK public opinion, particularly among under-35s, is towards support for decriminalisation of cannabis use (but not for other illegal drugs) though not necessarily full-scale legalisation. There is also widespread support among all age groups for doctors being able to prescribe cannabis to patients. Many commentators see politicians as lagging far behind public opinion.

### The key issues

The debate about the law on cannabis centres on a number of important legal and social issues concerning civil liberties and personal choice, legal coherence and international agreements. In addition, there are arguments about the link between cannabis and use of other drugs, whether law changes would increase or decrease drug problems and exactly what changes might take place.

Perhaps the most hotly debated social issue is that of civil liberties and personal choice. This argument hinges on the point at which it is appropriate to legislate to stop individuals from doing something that may do them harm and/or may result in substantial costs to society, even though such legislation is an infringement of personal choice.

Underlying this issue is fierce debate about exactly how dangerous cannabis use actually is. While some people see cannabis as a relatively harmless drug others see it as having detrimental impact on individual users and wider society.

The impact of criminalising otherwise law-abiding mainly young citizens, the detrimental impact on their future lives and careers (for example losing jobs or not being able

to work in jobs with children) and damage to the relationship between police and communities also need to be taken into account. Concerns over such issues were highlighted sharply by serious rioting in London.

### History

Cannabis was first documented as a herbal remedy in a Chinese pharmacy text of the first century AD. It was widely used in the Middle East, India and China as a medicine, to manufacture a range of products (such as clothes, rope and sacks), for religious ceremonies and for pleasure.

Cannabis was first introduced into Western medicine in the 1840s by a doctor who had been working in India. It was used for painkilling purposes particularly in childbirth and for period pains. Rumour has it that Queen Victoria was prescribed cannabis by her doctor. In the late 19th century and early part of this century cannabis was used by many people as a herbal remedy for a range of conditions.

Use of cannabis for pleasure also dates back to ancient China and India. The drug was brought to Western Europe by soldiers in Napoleon's army who had been fighting in north Africa at the beginning of the 19th century.

Non-medical use of cannabis was first banned in the UK in 1928 after South African and Egyptian delegates at an international conference about opium persuaded other countries that cannabis drove people mad.

*'Hashish absorbed in large quantities produces a furious delirium and... predisposes to acts of violence and produces a characteristic strident laugh... [With habitual use] the countenance of the addict becomes gloomy, his eye is wild, and the*

*expression of his face is stupid... his intellectual faculties gradually weaken and the whole organism decays. The addict very frequently becomes neurasthenic and eventually insane.'* – Dr El Guindy, Egyptian delegate, Second International Opium Conference, 1924.

This idea that cannabis drove people mad and that it led to them being out of control was popularised in the 1930s and 1940s in America by the head of the Narcotics Bureau, Harry Anslinger. He organised pamphlets, stories in magazines and newspapers and even a film called *Reefer Madness* to convince people that terrible crimes were committed by people who used cannabis.

At the time cannabis was hardly used in the UK and up to the mid 1960s its use was confined mainly to the London jazz scene and some West Indian communities. In the 1960s its use grew rapidly, especially among young university and college students. In 1973, as part of the introduction of the Misuse of Drugs Act, the government decided that cannabis had no medical uses and banned it being available on a doctor's prescription.

Although with the passing of the 1960s 'hippy' period, use of cannabis became less newsworthy, its actual use spread to other groups in society beyond middle-class students and media personalities. There was more attention for cannabis during the reggae boom of the mid 1970s and once again more recently on the back of the general rise in drug use among young people in the 1990s.

⇨ The above information is reprinted with kind permission from DrugScope. Visit www.drugscope. org.uk for more information.

© DrugScope

---

## Safety of drugs

**How safe are drugs? Largest percentage for each answer option.**

| Cannabis | Largest % | safe if used properly (only drug for which this is true) |
|---|---|---|
| Barbiturates | Largest % | never heard of it |
| Heroin/Ecstasy | Largest % | always unsafe |
| Poppers/Barbiturates | Largest % | heard but don't know much about it |

*Source:* Trends: Young People and Cannabis, 1987-2005, *from the Schools Health Education Unit (www.sheu.org.uk)*

# Cannabis information

## Information from HIT

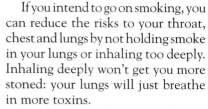

### Dependency

During the last few years it has become clear that cannabis use can result in dependency and lead to problems.

Some users become dependent on cannabis in a similar way to other drugs. Using it most days, over several months or more, can result in psychological dependency.

After smoking for an extended period, you may find you now need to smoke more than you used to, to get the same feeling even just to feel OK. People using cannabis heavily often say they have problems in various areas of their life – money worries, difficult relationships, conflict with family and friends, struggling to manage work or study commitments, ill-health – especially chest illnesses – and mental health problems such as depression, anxiety and schizophrenia.

In general, the symptoms of dependence are:
⇨ Using more, or for longer, than you meant to
⇨ A constant desire to use, or trying to give it up and failing
⇨ Spending a lot of time getting supplies, using and recovering
⇨ Spending less time on important activities or giving them up altogether

⇨ Keeping on using, even when you know it's harming you
⇨ Tolerance (needing more of the drug to get the same effect)
⇨ Withdrawal (unpleasant symptoms when you stop).

Are you spending too much time, energy and money on weed? Does a lot of your day revolve around dope? Do those close to you complain that you're stoned all the time?

Cannabis can lead to problems – could you stop if you wanted to?

### Smoking

Your lungs were not meant to take in hot, noxious gases, so smoking cannabis is bad for you.

If you smoke cannabis with tobacco, you expose your lungs to two harmful drugs and this increases the risks. Smoking can lead to illnesses like bronchitis, emphysema and cancer.

Many cannabis users also become long-term cigarette smokers. Giving up tobacco may be more difficult as a result of your cannabis use.

If you intend to go on smoking, you can reduce the risks to your throat, chest and lungs by not holding smoke in your lungs or inhaling too deeply. Inhaling deeply won't get you more stoned: your lungs will just breathe in more toxins.

Smoking cannabis can damage your health and other people's health too – show some respect and don't smoke around others, particularly children. Ideally, cut down and stop.

### Mental health

Have you ever felt tense or agitated after smoking pot? Have you ever had uncontrolled thoughts or become confused after a joint?

---

**Some people experience unpleasant effects when they use cannabis, such as anxiety, panic attacks or paranoia**

---

Some people experience unpleasant effects when they use cannabis, such as anxiety, panic attacks or paranoia. Usually these symptoms stop once the cannabis has worn off.

If you have had a mental health problem before or if you have a history of mental health problems in your family, cannabis can trigger serious mental health problems (such as schizophrenia). There is also concern that people who use cannabis a lot when they are young may be vulnerable to mental health problems later in life.

If you already have a mental health problem, cannabis will probably make your symptoms worse. Talk to your GP about any psychological and mental health issues.

If cannabis is affecting your mental health, stop using it.

*... IT IS CONSUMING MY LIFE...*

### Debt

One of the most common problems associated with cannabis is spending too much money on it!

Look at how much weed you're going through each week. Do you spend more than you intended to? How can you cut down the cost of your pot? Decide how much you can afford to spend and stick to it.

---

**The maximum sentence for possessing cannabis is 2 years in prison and an unlimited fine**

How much money do you spend on cannabis every week? Think what else you could buy with that amount of money.

### Relationships

Cannabis can make people boring, lifeless and isolated. Smoking dope all the time can lead to problems in both your personal life and at work.

⇨ Do you have a vibrant social life, or do you watch a lot of TV?
⇨ Is your partner giving you earache about your lack of motivation?
⇨ Have you lost interest in seeing friends?
⇨ Do you continue to smoke cannabis just because your partner does?

If you feel this is happening to you, cut down, use less often and stop.

### The law

Cannabis is a Class C drug. It is illegal and harmful. The maximum sentence for possessing cannabis is two years in prison and an unlimited fine. The maximum penalty for supplying cannabis is 14 years in prison and an unlimited fine.

People aged 18 and over are no longer automatically arrested for possessing cannabis. However, you will be arrested if:

⇨ You are caught regularly;
⇨ You smoke in public places;
⇨ You use cannabis near premises where children and young people go.

It is an offence to be in charge of a motor vehicle while under the influence of cannabis. Sentences include disqualification from driving, fines and imprisonment.

***If you are under 18 years of age***

People under 18 will still be arrested for possession of cannabis. This means the Police and the Youth Offending Team (YOT) can see if there are any underlying problems associated with a young person's cannabis use. The police can give reprimands and warnings at the police station – they will keep them on file in case the person is caught again. Offenders may end up in court in the future.

A criminal record can cause serious problems at home, college or work, and in later life.

⇨ Information from HIT. Visit www.knowcannabis.org.uk for more information.

*© HIT*

# Does cannabis lead to taking other drugs?

**Information from DrugScope**

This is the so-called 'escalation' hypothesis, or 'gateway theory'. In the mid-80s research from the US revived interest in this idea; specifically it was claimed that cannabis use tends to lead to heroin use, but the arguments are similar for progression to illicit drugs other than heroin.

---

**Most people who use heroin will have previously used cannabis**

Most people who use heroin will have previously used cannabis (though only a small proportion of those who try cannabis go on to use heroin). This could be because

cannabis actually does (at least for some people) lead to heroin use, but there are alternative explanations.

For instance, it could be that heroin and cannabis use are both caused by something else in the individual's personality or background that the researchers have not taken into account. Also the studies suggesting cannabis might lead to heroin have been done in Western societies at a time when cannabis is more freely available than heroin. This could

mean people tend to use cannabis first simply because they come across it first.

Even if cannabis use did lead to heroin use, there would remain the crucial issue of exactly how this happened. The assumption is that if cannabis leads to heroin, then more cannabis use would result in more heroin use – an argument against legalising cannabis. But the reverse could be the case. For instance, it could be that cannabis use involves people in the buying of illegal drugs, making it more likely that they will meet with an offer of heroin, an offer which some will accept. In this example it would be the illegality of cannabis use rather than cannabis use itself that led most directly to heroin use. The implication is that some heroin use might be prevented by legalising cannabis, even if this meant more widespread cannabis use.

This example illustrates the fact that the mechanism of any link between cannabis and heroin may be as important as whether or not such a link exists in the first place.

Recently a government report has concluded that cannabis does not lead to the use of other drugs. The report by the Home Office states that any gateway factors, where cannabis is seen as the gateway to other drugs, are 'too small to be a major factor'. The report *The Road to Ruin?* found that drug use is a consequence of lifestyle, of which cannabis, because it is more available, tends to be the first drug people encounter. The choice to take drugs like cocaine is a consequence of a person's predisposition to seeking and using drugs, not because they have taken any one type of drug.

⇨ The above information is reprinted with kind permission from DrugScope. Visit www.drugscope.org.uk for more information.
© *DrugScope*

# Reducing, or stopping, cannabis use

## Information from Release

### Drug treatment services

Conventional drug treatment services in the UK sometimes regard cannabis use as a low priority unless there is evidence of an underlying mental health problem. Young people's services tend to offer more help, but again the emphasis can be on mental health.

Nonetheless, local drug treatment services should be able to help users to reduce or stop cannabis use through a variety of techniques, including advice and support from a key worker and complementary therapies. Joining a local support group is a further option.

### Detoxing

Detoxing from cannabis use is not physically dangerous. However, medical advice should be sought if there are concerns about stopping use, particularly if cannabis is being used to relieve depression.

There will be limited physical discomfort when detoxing from cannabis. The main problems encountered are likely to include difficulties relaxing and lack of sleep. This can lead people to use other medication, such as tranquillisers, which are considerably more addictive.

Physical exercise can help increase natural endorphin levels and therefore assist with sleep. Complementary therapies, especially auricular acupuncture, can also

**RELEASE**

promote relaxation, as can herbal teas such as 'detox' tea, 'sleep' tea and 'lung' tea. These can be accessed through local drug treatment services, herbalists or alternative medicine outlets.

### Cognitive Behaviour Therapy

Elements of Cognitive Behaviour Therapy (CBT) can be applied to stopping cannabis use. CBT can be useful to help people learn to alter their responses to certain stimuli related to their drug use. This can help them to avoid risky situations or to take stock when their thought patterns drift towards using, by enabling them to implement learned coping strategies. This is particularly useful in avoiding ritualistic use, which can be a major obstacle to achieving abstinence.

### Peer pressure and the 'cool' factor

Peer pressure can be very influential on behaviour patterns, and the perception of drug use as being glamorous can lead people to experiment and form a habit. The provision of accurate, objective information will help people to make more informed choices about cannabis use.

⇨ Release is the national centre of expertise on drugs, the law and human rights, providing free legal services to the socially excluded. Release relies on charitable donations to continue its work – please go to www.release.org.uk if you would like to make a contribution.
© *Release*

I THOUGHT I WAS SUPPOSED TO FEEL 'COOL?'

# Drug misuse

## One in three young men use cannabis

In 2004/05, 14 per cent of men and eight per cent of women aged 16 to 59 in England and Wales said that they had taken an illicit drug in the previous year. Among young people (those aged 16 to 24), 33 per cent of men and 21 per cent of women said they had done so in the previous year.

The most commonly used drug by young people was cannabis, which had been used by 30 per cent of young men and 18 per cent of young women in the previous year.

### The most commonly used drug by young people was cannabis

Cocaine and ecstasy were the most commonly used Class A drugs In 2004/05, seven per cent of men and three per cent of women aged 16 to 24 had used cocaine in the previous year, and the same proportions reported use of ecstasy in the past year.

Since 1998 there has been an increase in the use of cocaine among young people. In contrast the use of cannabis, amphetamines and LSD has declined.

Drug offences accounted for three per cent of recorded crime in England and Wales in 2005/06. Drug offences can cover a range of activities, including unlawful production, supply, and most commonly, possession of illegal substances. Total recorded drug offences increased by 23 per cent in 2005/06 compared with 2004/05. The increase, for the most part, was due to a 36 per cent increase in the recording of possession of cannabis offences that coincided with an increase in the number of formal warnings for the possession of cannabis. This increase in formal warnings accounts for around two-thirds of the increase in cannabis possession offences.

In 2004, the latest year for which data are available, the total number of drug seizures in England and Wales declined by two per cent to 107,360. Seizures were 19,000 lower than in the last peak in 1998. HM Customs and the National Crime Squad generally seized larger amounts while local police forces made a greater number of smaller seizures.

Compared with 2003, in 2004 there were fewer Class A seizures (down 2%). Cannabis was reclassified from being a Class B to a Class C drug on 29 January 2004, and accounted for 70 per cent of the total number of seizures in 2004. Data for Classes B and C in 2004 are therefore distorted and should not be directly compared to those of earlier years.

In terms of the quantity of drugs seized, 4.6 tonnes of cocaine and 4.6 million tablets of ecstasy were seized in 2004, decreases of 33 per cent and 31 per cent respectively on 2003.

*Source:*
⇨ British Crime Survey 2004/05,
⇨ Crime in England and Wales 2005/06,
⇨ Seizures of drugs in England and Wales 2004, Home Office.
*Published on 16 August 2006*

⇨ Information from the Office for National Statistics. Visit www.statistics.gov.uk for more information.

© Crown copyright

# Vulnerability to hard drugs

## Information from *Neuropsychopharmacology*

The theory that experimentation with cannabis is harmless and won't lead to further drug use is challenged in an online publication in *Neuropsychopharmacology* this week.

Marijuana, often called a 'gateway' drug, is the most frequently used illegal drug by teens worldwide and previous research has shown that the adolescent brain is particularly sensitive to drug exposure. Gateway drugs is a term suggesting that addiction to one drug could make a person vulnerable to abuse and addiction of harder drugs.

The most common argument against the gateway drug theory is that adolescents move on to harder drugs because of peer and/or emotional pressures. Yasmin Hurd and colleagues demonstrate in animal models that cannabis can, in fact, affect future sensitivity to heroin. Studying neurobiological events after cannabis exposure, they found marijuana affects the human brain's natural chemicals called endogenous opioids, which are known to play a role in heightening positive emotions, and creating a sense of reward. This is the same system that is stimulated by hard drugs.

The team's results dispel the common belief that drug experimentation does not affect the brain. They show that the brain may 'remember' previous usage and make users vulnerable to harder drugs later in life.

This study may have an impact on governmental regulations calling for the legalisation of marijuana. And, any potential increase in the number of addicted people could impact healthcare, rehabilitation costs and crime rates.

*5 July 2006*

⇨ Reprinted by permission from Macmillan Publishers Ltd: *Neuropsychopharmacology* Volume 31, Issue 7, copyright 2006. Visit www.nature.com/npp for more information.

© Nature Publishing Group

# Public relaxed on the use of cannabis

**By Philip Johnston, Home Affairs Editor**

**M**ost people would be happy to see the personal use of cannabis decriminalised or penalties for possession lowered to the status of a parking fine, says one of the largest opinion surveys conducted on the issue.

The report showed that 700 annual hospital admissions on mental health grounds resulted from cannabis use.

However, the majority of the public is adamantly against any lessening of the restrictions on heroin or crack cocaine, drawing a clear distinction between so-called hard and soft drugs.

Three-quarters of people think that the sale and possession of hard drugs should remain a serious criminal offence but only a third think the same of soft drugs.

The YouGov survey, carried out for the *The Daily Telegraph* and the Royal Society for the Encouragement of Arts, Manufacturers and Commerce (RSA), indicates a pragmatic attitude towards drugs, legal and illegal, with many people acknowledging that the damage caused by alcohol and tobacco often outweighs that from the occasional use of soft drugs.

The findings follow a report this month from the Commons science and technology committee suggesting that the drugs classification system, which dates from 1971, should be scrapped and replaced by a scale that rates substances on the basis of health and social risks.

The committee proposed a scale that would rate substances purely on that basis, removing the link with potential punishments under the law.

The scale would include legal drugs, such as alcohol and tobacco, to give 'a better sense of the relative harm involved' in the consumption of drugs.

The Government is discussing new policies as part of a review of its 10-year drugs strategy, which runs out in 2008.

There is growing pressure on ministers to consider a new approach based on a 'rational' ranking of the harm that various substances cause.

The YouGov poll suggests that the public would be receptive to such a move.

Its findings will help to underpin the work of the RSA's commission on illegal drugs, communities and public policy, which has spent more than a year looking at the issue and will report in December.

## Asked which substances caused most harm, respondents placed tobacco and alcohol well ahead of cannabis and only just behind heroin

Asked which substances caused most harm, respondents placed tobacco and alcohol well ahead of cannabis and only just behind heroin.

That reflects the thinking of scientists who have drawn up a new scale based on risk which they say should replace the A, B and C rankings introduced in the Misuse of Drugs Act 35 years ago.

On this template, alcohol would be a borderline Class A/B drug because it is involved in more than half of all visits to accident and emergency departments and orthopaedic admissions. It often leads to violence and is a frequent cause of car accidents.

YouGov also confirms a sizeable age gap in attitudes to drugs: people born after 1960 are far more likely to regard their use as inevitable, whether or not they approve.

Government policy in recent years has been moving towards a tougher crackdown on hard drugs while encouraging the police to focus less, if at all, on the personal use of soft drugs such as cannabis.

That approach was behind the reclassification of cannabis and was reinforced by a recently published internal Whitehall study suggesting that most acquisitive crimes were committed by an estimated 280,000 high harm drug-users to support their cocaine and heroin habits. It found that the approach adopted over the past decade had failed to reduce hard drug use and the crime that accompanied it.

The study also said that more than three million people used illicit drugs every year and compared the 749 deaths annually from heroin and methadone with the 6,000 deaths from alcohol abuse and 100,000 from tobacco.

It also showed that about 700 annual hospital admissions on mental health grounds resulted from the use of cannabis, compared with 500 for heroin users.

*14 August 2006*

© Telegraph Group Limited 2006

# Cannabis and mental health

## Information from the Royal College of Psychiatrists

### About this article

Two million people in the UK smoke cannabis. Half of all 16- to 29-year-olds have tried it at least once. In spite of government warnings about health risks, many people see it as a harmless substance that helps you to relax and 'chill' – a drug that, unlike alcohol and cigarettes, might even be good for your physical and mental health. On the other hand, recent research has suggested that it can be a major cause of psychotic illnesses in those who are genetically vulnerable.

This article looks at the research on the effects of cannabis use and mental health and is for anyone who is concerned about the issue. We hope that this will help people to make informed choices about using – or not using – cannabis.

### What is cannabis?

*Cannabis sativa* and *cannabis indica* are members of the nettle family that have grown wild throughout the world for centuries. Both plants have been used for a variety of purposes including hemp to make rope and textiles, as a medical herb and as the popular recreational drug.

The plant is used as:
⇨ The resin – a brown/black lump , known as bhang, ganja, hashish, resin etc.;
⇨ The dried leaves – known as grass, marijuana, spliff, weed etc.

Skunk is one of the stronger types of cannabis which is grown especially for its higher concentration of psychoactive ingredients. It is named after the pungent smell it gives off during growing. It can be grown either under grow lights or in a greenhouse, often using hydroponic (growing in nutrient-rich liquids rather than soil) techniques. There are hundreds of other varieties of cannabis with exotic names such as AK-47 or Destroyer.

Street cannabis can come in a wide variety of strengths, so it is often not possible to judge exactly what is being used in any one particular session.

### How is it used?

Most commonly, the resin or the dried leaves are mixed with tobacco and smoked as a 'spliff' or 'joint'. The smoke is inhaled strongly and held in the lungs for a number of seconds. It can also be smoked in a pipe, a water pipe, or collected in a container before inhaling it – a 'bucket'. It can be brewed as tea or cooked in cakes.

More than half of its psychologically active chemical ingredients are absorbed into the blood when smoked. These compounds tend to build up in fatty tissues throughout the body, so it takes a long time to be excreted in the urine. This is why cannabis can be detected in urine up to 56 days after it has last been used.

### What is its legal status in the UK?

Before January 2004, it was classified as a Class B drug, alongside amphetamines and barbiturates. This dates from 1928, when Egyptian and South African doctors stated that heavy use could cause mental disturbances.

It is currently a Class C drug, in the same group as anabolic steroids and tranquillisers such as valium and temazepam. It is still illegal to have it and the maximum penalty for possession is two years.

The decision to reclassify cannabis was recently reconsidered by the Government's Advisory Council on the Misuse of Drugs (ACMD) because of worries about:
⇨ a possible connection with mental health problems;
⇨ the increased strength of the cannabis that is now widely used.

However, the decision was taken in January 2006 to keep it as a Class C drug under the Misuse of Drugs Act, 1971.

This means that the maximum penalties are:
⇨ For possession: 2-year prison sentence or an unlimited fine, or both;
⇨ For dealing/supplying: 14-year prison sentence or an unlimited fine, or both.

### How does it work and what is the chemical make-up of cannabis?

There are about 60 compounds and 400 chemicals in an average cannabis plant. The four main compounds are called delta-9-tetrahydrocannabinol (delta-9-THC), cannabidiol, delta-8-tetrahydrocannabinol and cannabinol. Apart from cannabidiol (CBD), these compounds are psychoactive, the strongest one being delta-9-tetrahydrocannabinol. The stronger varieties of the plant contain little cannabidiol (CBD), whilst the delta-9-THC content is a lot higher.

When cannabis is smoked, its compounds rapidly enter the bloodstream and are transported directly to the brain and other parts of the body. The feeling of being 'stoned' or 'high' is caused mainly by the delta-9-THC binding to cannabinoid receptors in the brain. A receptor is a site or brain cell where certain substances can stick or 'bind' for a while. If this happens, it has an effect on the cell and the nerve impulses it produces. Curiously, there are also cannabis-like substances produced naturally by the brain itself – these are called endocannabinoids.

Most of these receptors are found in the parts of the brain that influence pleasure, memory, thought, concentration, sensory and time perception. Cannabis compounds can also affect the eyes, the ears, the skin and the stomach.

### What are its effects?
*Pleasant*
A 'high' – a sense of relaxation, happiness, sleepiness, colours appear more intense, music sounds better.

---

**Two million people in the UK smoke cannabis. Half of all 16- to 29-year-olds have tried it at least once**

---

*Unpleasant*
Around one in 10 cannabis users have unpleasant experiences, including confusion, hallucinations, anxiety and paranoia. The same person may have either pleasant or unpleasant effects depending on their mood and circumstances. These feelings are usually only temporary – although as the drug can stay in the system for some weeks, the effect can be more long-lasting than users realise. Long-term use can have a depressant effect, reducing motivation.
*Education and learning*
There have also been suggestions that cannabis may interfere with a person's capacity to:
⇨ concentrate;
⇨ organise information;
⇨ use information.

This effect seems to last several weeks after use, which can cause particular problems for students.

However, a large study in New Zealand followed up 1,265 children for 25 years. It found that cannabis use in adolescence was linked to poor school performance, but that there was no direct connection between the two. It looked as though

it was simply because cannabis use encouraged a way of life that didn't help with schoolwork.

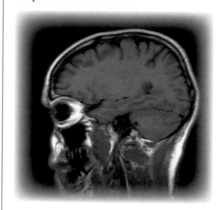
Does cannabis damage mental health?

*Work*
It seems to have a similar effect on people at work. There is no evidence that cannabis causes specific health hazards. But users are more likely to leave work without permission, spend work time on personal matters or simply daydream. Cannabis users themselves report that drug use has interfered with their work and social life.

Of course, some areas of work are more demanding than others. A review of the research on the effect of cannabis on pilots revealed that those who had used cannabis made far more mistakes, both major and minor, than when they had not smoked cannabis. As you can imagine, the pilots were tested in flight simulators, not actually flying ...

The worst effects were in the first four hours, although they persisted for at least 24 hours, even when the pilot had no sense at all of being 'high'. It concluded 'Most of us, with this evidence, would not want to fly with a pilot who had smoked cannabis within the last day or so'.
*What about driving?*
In New Zealand, researchers found that those who smoked regularly, and had smoked before driving, were more likely to be injured in a car crash. A recent study in France looked at over 10,000 drivers who were involved in fatal car crashes. Even when the influence of alcohol was taken into account, cannabis users were more than twice as likely to be the cause of a fatal crash than to be one of the victims. So – perhaps most of us would also not want to be

driven by somebody who had smoked cannabis in the last day or so.
*Mental health problems*
There is growing evidence that people with serious mental illness, including depression and psychosis, are more likely to use cannabis or have used it for long periods of time in the past. Regular use of the drug has appeared to double the risk of developing a psychotic episode or long-term schizophrenia. However, does cannabis cause depression and schizophrenia or do people with these disorders use it as a medication?

Over the past few years, research has strongly suggested that there is a clear link between early cannabis use and later mental health problems in those with a genetic vulnerability – and that there is a particular issue with the use of cannabis by adolescents.
*Depression*
A study following 1,600 Australian school-children, aged 14 to 15 for seven years, found that while children who use cannabis regularly have a significantly higher risk of depression, the opposite was not the case – children who already suffered from depression were not more likely than anyone else to use cannabis. However, adolescents who used cannabis daily were five times more likely to develop depression and anxiety in later life.
*Schizophrenia*
Three major studies followed large numbers of people over several years, and showed that those people who use cannabis have a higher than average risk of developing schizophrenia. If you start smoking it before the age of 15, you are 4 times more likely to develop a psychotic disorder by the time you are 26. They found no evidence of self-medication. It seemed that, the more cannabis someone used, the more likely they were to develop symptoms.

Why should teenagers be particularly vulnerable to the use of cannabis? No one knows for certain, but it may be something to do with brain development. The brain is still developing in the teenage years – up to the age of around 20, in fact. A massive process of 'neural pruning' is going on. This is rather like streamlining a tangled jumble of circuits so they can work more effectively. Any experience, or substance, that affects this process has the potential to produce long-term psychological effects.

Recent research in Europe, and in the UK, has suggested that people who have a family background of mental illness – so probably have a genetic vulnerability anyway – are more likely to develop schizophrenia if they use cannabis as well.

### Is there such a thing as 'cannabis psychosis'?

Recent research in Denmark suggests that yes, there is. It is a short-lived psychotic disorder that seems to be brought on by cannabis use but which subsides fairly quickly once the individual has stopped using it. It's quite unusual though – in the whole of Denmark they found only around 100 new cases per year.

However, they also found that:
⇨ Three-quarters had a different psychotic disorder diagnosed within the next year;
⇨ Nearly half still had a psychotic disorder three years later.

So, it also seems probable that nearly half of those diagnosed as having cannabis psychosis are actually showing the first signs of a more long-lasting psychotic disorder, such as schizophrenia. It may be this group of people who are particularly vulnerable to the effects of cannabis, and so should probably avoid it in the future.

### Is cannabis addictive?

It has some of the features of addictive drugs such as:
⇨ tolerance – having to take more and more to get the same effect;
⇨ withdrawal symptoms. These have been shown in heavy users and include:
   ↳ craving
   ↳ decreased appetite
   ↳ sleep difficulty
   ↳ weight loss
   ↳ aggression, anger, irritability, restlessness, and strange dreams.

These symptoms of withdrawal produce about the same amount of discomfort as withdrawing from tobacco.

For regular, long-term users:
⇨ 3 out of 4 experience cravings;
⇨ half become irritable;

⇨ seven out of 10 switch to tobacco in an attempt to stay off cannabis.

The irritability, anxiety and problems with sleeping usually appear 10 hours after the last joint, and peak at around one week after the last use of the drug.

### Compulsive use

The user feels they have to have it and spends much of their life seeking, buying and using it. They cannot stop even when other important parts of their life (family, school, work) suffer.

You are most likely to become dependent on cannabis if you use it every day.

## What about skunk and other stronger varieties?

Traditional herbal cannabis contains between one and 15 per cent of the main psycho-active ingredient, THC. Some of the newer strains, including skunk, contain up to 20 per cent, so can be three times as strong as traditional cannabis. It works more quickly, and can produce hallucinations with profound relaxation and elation – along with nervousness, anxiety attacks, projectile vomiting and a strong desire to eat. They may be used by some as a substitute for Ecstasy or LSD.

Legally, these strains remain classified Class C drugs. While there is little research so far, it is likely that these stronger strains carry a higher risk of causing mental illness. A major

study currently under way has already reported problems with concentration and short-term memory in users of stronger types of cannabis.

## Problems with cannabis use

Many – perhaps most – people who use cannabis do enjoy it. But it can become a problem for some people. A US organisation, marijuana-anonymous.org, defines the problems of cannabis as follows:

'…if cannabis controls our lives and our thinking, and if our desires centre around marijuana – scoring it, dealing it, and finding ways to stay high so that we lose interest in all else.'

The website carries the following questionnaire – which could equally well apply to alcohol use.

'If you answer "Yes" to any of the questions, you may have a problem.

1. Has smoking pot stopped being fun?
2. Do you ever get high alone?
3. Is it hard for you to imagine a life without marijuana?
4. Do you find that your friends are determined by your marijuana use?
5. Do you smoke marijuana to avoid dealing with your problems?
6. Do you smoke pot to cope with your feelings?
7. Does your marijuana use let you live in a privately defined world?
8. Have you ever failed to keep promises you made about cutting down or controlling your dope smoking?
9. Has marijuana caused problems with memory, concentration, or motivation?
10. When your stash is nearly empty, do you feel anxious or worried about how to get more?
11. Do you plan your life around your marijuana use?
12. Have friends or relatives ever complained that your pot smoking is damaging your relationship with them?'

⇨ The above information is reprinted with kind permission from the Royal College of Psychiatrists. Visit www.rcpsych.ac.uk for more information.

*© Royal College of Psychiatrists*

# Cannabis and problem behaviour

## Cannabis linked to problem behaviour in secondary school children

A new Dutch study published in the February issue of the *British Journal of Psychiatry*, found that cannabis use is associated with 'externalising' problems (delinquent and aggressive behaviour), but not with 'internalising' problems (withdrawn behaviour and depression).

The strength of the link increased with higher use of cannabis, and significant associations were present only among those who had used cannabis recently. Lifetime cannabis users, who had not taken the drug in the past year, were not at higher risk than those who had never used cannabis. The study set out to investigate the link between cannabis use and mental health among Dutch adolescents.

Information about 5,551 young people aged 12-16 was drawn from the Dutch *Health Behaviour in School-Aged Children* survey, which was carried out as part of the international 2001 World Health Organisation project.

All participants in the study completed anonymous questionnaires that measured mental health and cannabis use, and also took into account possible confounding factors, such as smoking and alcohol use, which might have affected the results.

Among heavy cannabis users an association with thought and attention problems was found. Those using cannabis reported lower-than-average school performance significantly more often than those who did not use cannabis (13% v. 4%).

It is notable that regular cigarette smoking, which may be considered more 'normal' behaviour than cannabis use, explained a substantial part of the association between cannabis and delinquent and aggressive behaviour.

This may possibly be due to common risk factors. It may also be that regular smoking is accepted behaviour for adults but not for adolescents. Therefore, regular smoking, like cannabis use, might also be a way for adolescents to show their rebelliousness.

Although no association between cannabis and internalising problems was found, this does not rule out the possibility that there is a small group of vulnerable young people using the drug who are at increased risk of, for example, depression.

The authors of the study comment that despite the fact that cannabis use is not illegal in the Netherlands, use of the drug in adolescence is disapproved of by parents there, making it part of a deviant behaviour pattern in Holland as in other countries.

Furthermore, the strong confounding effects of alcohol use and smoking show that cannabis use is not a unique factor, but is one of several substances related to mental health problems.

### References

Monshouwer K, Van Dorsselaer S, Verdurmen J, Ter Bogt T, De Graaf R and Volleberbergh W (2006) Cannabis use and mental health in secondary school children: Findings from a Dutch survey. *British Journal of Psychiatry*, 188, 148-153.
*1 February 2006*

⇨ The above information is reprinted with kind permission from the Royal College of Psychiatrists. Visit www.rcpsych.ac.uk for more information.

© *Royal College of Psychiatrists*

# Cannabis and lung cancer

## The big dope debate

**By Jaspre Bark**

Since it first became the target of sensational media coverage in the last century, many evil effects have been claimed of cannabis use. These have included unstoppable homicidal rage, unchecked sexual mania and complete mental decline. At the height of the 'reefer madness' scare of the 1930s, American Drugs Czar Harry Anslinger was reported to have said: 'If the hideous monster Frankenstein came face to face with the monster marijuana he would drop dead of fright.'

> **There is still a debate raging in the medical community over whether there is any link between lung cancer and smoking cannabis**

However, one recent health scare associated with cannabis use has very sobering connotations, its alleged link to lung cancer. There is still a wide-scale debate raging in the medical community over whether there is any link between lung cancer and smoking cannabis. No overwhelming proof of this link has been discovered and a general conclusion has yet to be reached.

The main problem lies in the fact that most people who smoke cannabis do so in conjunction with tobacco, which is known to be carcinogenic. Cannabis smokers also hold the smoke in their lungs for much longer to obtain the maximum hit from the smoke, which could put them at greater risk to any pollutants in the smoke.

Dr Marinel Ammenheuser and her colleagues at the University of Texas Medical Branch studied a group of pregnant women who only smoked cannabis. They claim to have discovered evidence that cannabis smoking causes the same kind of damage to DNA as tobacco. 'We did a test to detect changes in a particular gene in the DNA in their white blood cells, and found that the marijuana smokers had three times as many DNA damaged cells as the non-smokers,' Dr Ammenheuser states. She held that a group of chemicals called poly-aromatic hydrocarbons are responsible. Similarly Dr Michael Roth discovered preliminary evidence that THC, the psychoactive ingredient in cannabis, may promote a carcinogenic effect.

This would seem to be in direct contradiction to the findings of Dr Louis Harris from the Medical College of Virginia though, who discovered that delta-8 THC, delta-9 THC and cannabinol (all components of THC) are quite active as anti-cancer agents.

There is also controversy surrounding what makes tobacco smoke carcinogenic. Tobacco companies have held for years that it is tar, adhering to lesions on the lung caused by smoke damage, that causes cancer. However, there is a body of evidence which suggests that it is radioactive elements within the chemical fertilisers used on tobacco plants that cause cancer. The phosphates used in the fertilisers are rich in radium 226 which breaks down into two daughter elements: lead 210 and polonium 210, which each have a huge half-life (they stay toxic for a very long time). These radioactive particles become airborne, and attach themselves to the fine hairs on tobacco leaves.

A vast number of studies have linked these particles, and their high incidence in the lungs of cancer victims, with the causes of cancer in those who smoke. As no phosphate is used in the fertilisation of cannabis, campaigners argue that it is free from radioactive particles and thereby not carcinogenic, at least not in the same way.

Without any conclusive proof on either side of the argument, the debate continues.

⇨ The above information is reprinted with kind permission from TheSite.org. For more information, please visit their website at www.thesite.org

© TheSite.org

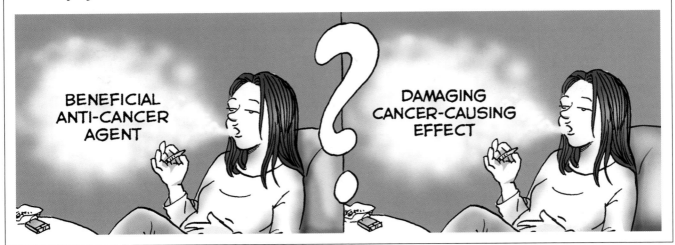

BENEFICIAL ANTI-CANCER AGENT

DAMAGING CANCER-CAUSING EFFECT

# A smoking gun?

## The impact of cannabis smoking on respiratory health

### Introduction

Cannabis is the most widely consumed illegal drug in the UK. Recent media coverage has focused on the public and political debate around issues such as reclassification of cannabis and how the police should deal with those who sell or are found to be in possession of varying amounts of the substance.

What has been consistently missing from the public debate on the safety or otherwise of cannabis as compared to other illegal drugs is the impact of smoking cannabis on respiratory health and the possible link with nicotine addiction in the form of tobacco smoking.

This report sets out to identify existing scientific and medical research on cannabis smoking and respiratory health. It identifies what conclusions it is possible to draw from the existing evidence and highlights gaps in our knowledge which require further research.

The aim of this report is to ensure that those taking part in the debate on cannabis and those engaged in promoting health education to our young people have the fullest possible information on the medical and scientific evidence of the impact of cannabis smoking on respiratory health.

## BRITISH LUNG FOUNDATION

Many young people will make decisions about whether they wish to use cannabis or not – regardless of its legal status. We have a duty to ensure that they do so with full knowledge of the risks associated with smoking cannabis.

### Summary of findings and recommendations

While there is a wealth of research into the health impact of tobacco smoking, there is relatively little on the effects of cannabis smoking.

Research investigating whether the inhalation of cannabis smoke causes damage to the lungs and airways focuses on whether this effect is independent of the effects of tobacco smoke or not. In general, the studies indicate that there is an increased negative health impact on those who smoke cannabis compared to those who do not smoke at all. When cannabis is smoked together with tobacco then the effects are additive. However, what is not clear is whether it is the addition of the cannabis or the tobacco which is more harmful or whether this is the result of the combined effects of equally harmful substances.

---

**3-4 cannabis cigarettes a day are associated with the same evidence of acute and chronic bronchitis and the same degree of damage to the bronchial mucosa as 20 or more tobacco cigarettes a day**

---

Some key findings emerge from the research:

⇨ The cannabis smoked today is much more potent that that smoked in the 1960s. The average cannabis cigarette smoked in the 1960s contained about 10mg of tetrahydrocannabinol (THC), the ingredient which accounts for the psychoactive properties of cannabis, compared to 150mg of THC today. This means that longitudinal studies carried out in the 1960s and 1970s may not be indicative of the effects of cannabis cigarettes smoked today.

⇨ Studies comparing the clinical effects of habitual cannabis smokers versus non-smokers demonstrate a significantly higher prevalence of chronic and acute respiratory symptoms such as chronic cough and sputum production, wheeze and acute bronchitis episodes.

⇨ 3-4 cannabis cigarettes a day are associated with the same evidence of acute and chronic bronchitis and the same degree of damage to the bronchial mucosa as 20 or more tobacco cigarettes a day.

CANNABIS STAR

Continued use causes chronic cough, bad breath, and bronchitis.

100% home grown

FUTURE GOVERNMENT HEALTH WARNING

- Cannabis tends to be smoked in a way which increases the puff volume by two-thirds and depth of inhalation by one-third. There is an average fourfold longer breath-holding time with cannabis than with tobacco. This means that there is a greater respiratory burden of carbon monoxide and smoke particulates such as tar than when smoking a similar quantity of tobacco.
- Cannabis smoking is likely to weaken the immune system. Infections of the lung are due to a combination of smoking-related damage to the cells lining the bronchial passage (the fine hair-like projection on these cells filter out inhaled microorganisms) and impairment of the principal immune cells in the small air sacs caused by cannabis.
- The evidence concerning a possible link between cannabis smoking and Chronic Obstructive Pulmonary Disease (COPD) has not yet been conclusively established. A number of studies indicate a causal relationship between the two whereas others contradict these findings.
- Research linking cannabis smoking to the development of respiratory cancer exists although there have also been conflicting findings. Not only does the tar in a cannabis cigarette contain many of the same known carcinogens as tobacco smoke but the concentrations of these are up to 50% higher in the smoke of a cannabis cigarette. It also deposits four times as much tar on the respiratory tract as an unfiltered cigarette of the same wieght. Smokers of cannabis and tobacco have shown a greater increase in cellular abnormalities indicating a cumulative effect of smoking both.
- The THC in cannabis has been shown to have a short-term bronchodilator effect. This has led to suggestions that THC may have therapeutic benefits in asthma. However, the noxious gases, chronic airway irritation or malignancy after long-term use associated with smoking would seem likely to negate these benefits.

## The cannabis smoked today is much more potent that that smoked in the 1960s

### Recommendations

From a clinical perspective the main effects of smoking cannabis on the lungs are increased risk of pulmonary infections and respiratory cancers. Benzpyrene, a known constituent of the tar of cannabis cigarettes, has been shown to promote alterations in one of the most common tumour suppressor genes, p53, hence facilitating the development of respiratory cancer. Gene p53 is thought to play a role in 75% of all lung cancers.

The British Lung Foundation recommends a public health education campaign aimed at young people to ensure that they are fully aware of the increased risk of pulmonary infections and respiratory cancers associated with cannabis smoking.

## Cannabis tends to be smoked in a way which increases the puff volume by two-thirds and depth of inhalation by one-third

The increased potency of the cannabis smoked today compared to the cannabis smoked twenty-thirty years ago suggests that earlier studies may underestimate the effects of cannabis smoking. In addition the lack of conclusive evidence concerning the link between cannabis smoking and Chronic Obstructive Pulmonary Disease (COPD) underlines the need for further research.

The British Lung Foundation recommends that further research is undertaken to take into account the increased potency of today's cannabis and to establish what link (if any) there is between COPD and cannabis smoking.

- The above information is an extract from the British Lung Foundation report *A smoking gun? The impact of cannabis smoking on respiratory health.* Reproduced by kind permission. The British Lung Foundation is the only UK charity working for everyone affected by lung disease. Helpline 08458 50 50 20, website www.lunguk.org.

*© British Lung Foundation (Registered charity no. 326730)*

# Drug testing at work

## You don't have to resign in a blind panic, but you do need to know where you stand

### You are what you wee

Your body attempts to break down anything you shove inside it, from food to drink and drugs. 'Metabolites' are formed as part of this process, and testing looks for specific types that could only occur as a result of drug taking and can remain inside the body for long periods.

---

**If a tester had to nominate the most easily-detectable drug, it would probably be cannabis**

### High times? Testing times

If a tester had to nominate the most easily-detectable drug, it would probably be cannabis. The active ingredient in cannabis is called THC, and the metabolites from THC can take weeks to clear the body, depending on your body size and drug habit. As a non water-soluble substance, you can't flush THC from your system overnight. Instead, it tends to get caught up in the body and released at a much slower rate. Smoking a joint a couple of nights a week may take 21-28 days to clear the system. Heavy cannabis use may be detected in the system up to 42-56 days later.

Here's a rough guide to some other drug metabolites that outstay their welcome, and which a urine test won't miss:
⇨ 2-4 days: Amphetamines, cocaine, ecstasy, heroin and other opiates.
⇨ 1-7 days: Barbiturates.

### Other tests

Drug metabolites can be also be detected in blood, perspiration and other body residue, but hair is an increasingly popular testing ground. Why? Because metabolites can supposedly filter out with hair growth and resist pretty much everything

TheSite.org

from shampooing to perm jobs. Testing involves dissolving the hair sample in a series of solvents that extract the drug metabolites.

### Can it be dodged?

Short of shaving your head, or having a ready supply of infant wee to hand, there is no sure-fire means. There are many products on the market that claim to beat the test, mostly by adding masking substances to your urine sample. However, the means of detection is becoming increasingly sophisticated, so what might work one day might fail badly the next.

The legal position for drug testing is complicated. It's acknowledged that employers have a justifiable interest in employees' drug use in certain circumstances. These include employees using drugs or alcohol in the workplace, or if drug or alcohol use is affecting your performance or

safety at work. But the principles behind current measures also state that people are entitled to a private life and dignity. A drug test shouldn't be imposed on you, and should only be introduced after a consultation and in good faith.

### But I'm innocent!

There's lots of debate over the accuracy of drug test results. If you really haven't taken drugs and your test comes back positive, it's time to have a serious talk with your boss, and if they're not listening, get some legal support.

Testing positive for drugs doesn't automatically mean dismissal. Your employer may decide to shift you to another part of the company if safety is an issue. They may even offer you help and support, especially if you're more than a recreational user. The best ammunition against a positive result is to be a star employee that they just can't live without!

⇨ The above information is re-printed with kind permission from TheSite.org. Visit www.thesite.org for more information.

© TheSite.org

# The state of the cannabis problem in Europe

## An extract from the European Monitoring Centre for Drugs and Drug Addiction's *Annual Report 2005*

### Prevalence and patterns

Cannabis is by far the most commonly used illegal substance in Europe. Recent population surveys indicate that between 3% and 31% of adults (aged 15 to 64 years) have tried the substance at least once (lifetime use). The lowest prevalence rates of lifetime use are found in Malta (3.5%), Portugal (7.6%) and Poland (7.7%) and the highest in France (26.2%), the United Kingdom (30.8%) and Denmark (31.3%). In most countries (15 of 23 countries with information) lifetime prevalence lies between 10% and 25%.

Between 1% and 11% of adults report having used cannabis in the last 12 months, with Malta, Greece and Sweden presenting the lowest prevalence rates and the Czech Republic, France, Spain and the United Kingdom the highest. Most countries (14) reported prevalence rates of recent use of between 3% and 7%.

An estimate of the total number of adults (15 to 64 years) using cannabis in the EU as a whole can be constructed from the available

European Monitoring Centre for Drugs and Drug Addiction

national estimates. This exercise suggests that around 20% of the total population, or over 62 million people, have ever tried cannabis. This figure falls to around 6% of adults, or in excess of 20 million people, when the more recent use of cannabis is considered (last year prevalence). For comparison, in the 2003 United States national survey on drug use and health (SAMHSA, 2003), 40.6% of adults (defined as 12 years and older) reported having tried cannabis or marijuana at least once and 10.6% reported having used it during the previous 12 months. Among 18- to 25-year-olds, the figures were 53.9% (lifetime), 28.5% (last 12 months) and 17% (last month)[3].

As is the case with other drugs, young adults consistently report higher rates of use. Between 11%

and 44% of young Europeans aged 15 to 34 years report that they have ever tried cannabis, with the lowest prevalence rates being found in Greece, Portugal and Poland and the highest in France (39.9%), the United Kingdom (43.4%) and Denmark (44.6%). Recent use was reported by 3-22% of young adults, with the lowest figures in Greece, Sweden, Poland and Portugal, and the highest in the United Kingdom (19.5%), France (19.7%), and the Czech Republic (22.1%) and 11 countries reporting recent use prevalence rates of between 7%

### Between 1% and 11% of adults report having used cannabis in the last 12 months

and 15%. Among 15- to 24-year-old Europeans, 9-45% claim to have tried cannabis, with rates in most countries falling in the range 20-35%. Recent use (in the last 12 months) was reported by 4-32%, with rates in most countries being in the range 9-21%[4].

### Estimating drug use in the population

Drug use in the general population is assessed through surveys, which provide estimates of the proportion of the population that has used drugs over defined periods of time: lifetime use (experimentation), last 12 months' use (recent use) or last 30 days' use (current use).[1]

The EMCDDA has developed a set of common core items ('European model questionnaire', EMQ) that is implemented in, or compatible with, most surveys in the EU Member

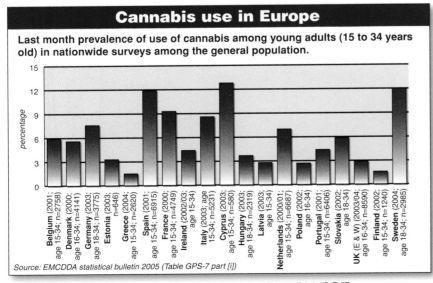

**Cannabis use in Europe**

Last month prevalence of use of cannabis among young adults (15 to 34 years old) in nationwide surveys among the general population.

*Source: EMCDDA statistical bulletin 2005 (Table GPS-7 part [i])*

ST. MARY'S UNIVERSITY COLLEGE

A COLLEGE OF THE QUEEN'S UNIVERSITY OF BELFAST

States. The EMQ is included in a report available on the EMCDDA website.[2] 'Lifetime use' may be of limited value as an indicator of the current situation among adults (although it could be a reasonable indicator among school children), but in conjunction with other measures it can give insight into aspects of patterns of use (continuation or discontinuation of use) and the generational dynamics of the spread of drug use. 'Last 12 months' use' gives an indication of recent drug use, although often this use will be occasional, and 'last 30 days' use' gives an indication of more current use, which will include people using the drug frequently.

As with other illicit drugs, rates of cannabis use are notably higher among males than among females, although the extent of this difference varies between countries. The male-female ratio for lifetime experience varies from 1.25:1 to 4:1 (1.25 to 4 men for each woman) and for current use from approximately 2:1 to 6:1. Surveys also indicate that cannabis use is more common in urban areas or in areas with high population density. Thus, national differences noted might, in part, reflect differences in levels of urbanisation, although it has been suggested that recreational drug use is spreading from urban areas towards rural areas.

The fact that rates of recent use and current use are substantially lower than lifetime experience rates indicates that cannabis use tends to be occasional, or to be discontinued after some time. In most EU countries, 20-40% of those adults who have ever tried cannabis report having used it during the previous 12 months, and about 10-20% report having used it during the last 30 days ('continuation rates').

---

## A very rough estimation will be that one in 10 to 20 young Europeans is a current user of cannabis

---

In recent surveys, rates of use in the last month were reported by 0.5-9% of all adults (with many countries in the range 2-4%), by 1.5-13% of young adults (with many countries in the range 3-8%) and by 1.2-16% of 15- to 24-year-olds (with many countries in the range 5-10%). A very rough estimation will be that one in 10 to 20 young Europeans is a current user of cannabis. The countries with the lowest current prevalence rates included Malta, Greece, Sweden, Poland and Finland, while the United Kingdom and Spain had the highest.

In the 2004 annual report (EMCDDA, 2004a), data presented on frequency of cannabis use in the last 30 days suggested that approximately one-quarter (19-33%) of those who had used cannabis in the last month were doing so on a daily or almost daily basis,[5] most of them young males. It was estimated that among 15- to 34-year-old Europeans, 0.9-3.7% were daily cannabis users, and that roughly 3 million people in Europe could be using the substance daily or almost daily.

### Notes

1. For more about the methodology of population surveys, and the methodology used in each national survey, see the 2005 statistical bulletin.
2. Handbook for surveys about drug use among the general population (http://www.emcdda.eu.int/?nnodeid=1380).
3. Note that the age range in the US survey (12 years and over) is wider than the age range reported by the EMCDDA for EU surveys (15-64 years). On the other hand, the age range for young adults (18-25 years) is narrower than the range used in most EU surveys (15-24 years).
4. See Figure GPS-2 in the 2005 statistical bulletin.
5. See the 2004 annual report (http://ar2004.emcdda.eu.int). The information refers to 'use on 20 days or more during the past 30 days', expressed also as 'daily or almost daily use'.

⇨ An overview of cannabis potency in Europe, European Monitoring Centre for Drugs and Drug Addiction (EMCDDA), 2006. Taken from the *Annual Report 2005*. Visit www.emcdda.europa.eu for more information or to view the full report.

© EMCDDA

# The cannabis market – production

**Information taken from the *2006 World Drug Report***

Production of cannabis basically comprises three different products: cannabis herb, cannabis resin and cannabis oil.

⇨ Cannabis herb is composed of the flowering tops and leaves of the plant, which are smoked like tobacco using a variety of techniques. While this drug is consumed throughout the world, the largest market for cannabis herb is in the Americas, accounting for more than 60 per cent of global seizures in 2004. North America alone was responsible for more than half of all seizures. Africa accounted for more than 30 per cent of global cannabis herb seizures. Over the 1994-2004 period, the proportion of cannabis herb seizures in global cannabis seizures amounted to 79 per cent (81 per cent in 2004).

⇨ Cannabis resin (hashish) consists of the secretions of the plant emitted in the flowering phase of its development. Nineteen per cent of global cannabis seizures were in the form of cannabis resin in 2004. Western Europe is the largest market for cannabis resin, accounting for more than 70 per cent of global resin seizures in 2004, and some 80 per cent of the hashish consumed in Europe is estimated to be produced in Morocco.

⇨ Cannabis oil (hashish oil) is far less widely used than cannabis herb or cannabis resin. Although cannabis oil seizures doubled in 2004, they accounted still for just 0.01 per cent of global cannabis seizures in 2004.

---

## Production of cannabis basically composes three different products: cannabis herb, cannabis resin and cannabis oil

---

Production estimates for cannabis are collected by UNODC, but must be regarded with a high degree of caution. They are highly tentative and should be viewed as informed guesses established by experts. As scientifically valid monitoring systems for cannabis cultivation continue to be the exception and not the rule, even major producing countries are not in a position to provide scientifically valid estimates.

Moreover, the fact that cannabis is a plant that grows in virtually every inhabited region of the world, that can be cultivated with little maintenance on small plots, and that can even be grown indoors, further complicates matters. Therefore, remote sensing approaches in estimating the areas under cultivation, as used for poppy and coca, are difficult if not impossible if global cultivation had to be estimated.

In other words, the lack of clear geographical concentrations in a few countries (as is the case for opium poppy or cocaine) has made it difficult to introduce effective and reliable crop monitoring systems for the world at large.

### Cannabis herb is cultivated in some 176 countries

Over the 1994-2004 period, 82 countries provided UNODC with cannabis production estimates. For comparison, only 36 countries provided estimates for opium poppy cultivation, and only six provided estimates for coca leaf production.

The fact that a country did not provide an estimate does not mean that no cultivation exists, as many countries lack the capacity to establish reliable estimates. Another possibility to identify cannabis-producing countries has been to analyse reports on the source of the cannabis trafficked in a country. On this basis, 142 producer countries could be identified for the 1994-2004 period.

A third list of producer countries was generated by singling out those that report the seizure of whole cannabis plants. It is inefficient and thus unlikely to transport whole plants internationally, as only certain parts are useable as a drug. Thus, when a whole plant is seized, it is very likely that it was locally produced. Seizures of whole cannabis plants were reported in 141 countries during the 1994-2004 period.

Combining these three lists results in the identification of 176 countries and territories where cannabis is produced. This is equivalent to 90 per cent of the countries and territories which receive UNODC's Annual Reports Questionnaire (195). However, there are no indications that in the remaining countries cannabis production does not take place.

### Global production of cannabis is estimated at 45,000 metric tons

Since the publication of the *2005 World Drug Report*, there has been a slight increase in the global cannabis production estimate, from 42,000 metric tons to 45,000 metric tons. A tentative breakdown of these estimates shows that the bulk of cannabis continues to be produced in the Americas (54 per cent), notably in North America (35 per cent), in South America (18 per cent), Africa (27 per cent) and Asia (15 per cent). Only 4 per cent of global cannabis herb production occurs in Europe. This may appear low, however, it should be noted that Europe also accounts for just three per cent of global cannabis herb seizures. Oceania accounts for 1 per cent of global production.

### Production of herbal cannabis in North America appears to decline

A number of indicators suggest that the Americas, and notably North America, produce more cannabis than any other region. The cannabis markets in the Americas are, however, largely self-sufficient, that is, most of the cannabis produced in the Americas is also consumed in the region.

According to United States estimates, 10,100 metric tons of cannabis herb were produced in Mexico in 2005. This would make Mexico the largest cannabis herb producer in North America. In the United States, about 4,455 metric tons of cannabis herb were produced in 2004/5, according to the United States Office of National Drug Control Policy. An estimated 800 metric tons of cannabis herb are produced in Canada. Cannabis herb production in that region appears to have declined. In Mexico, production of cannabis herb is said to have decreased from 13,500 metric tons in 2003 to 10,100 metric tons in 2005 (-25 per cent). This success was largely due to large-scale eradication efforts. Similarly, in the United States production has been reduced from some 5,560 metric tons to 4,455 metric tons.

### Cannabis production significantly increases in Paraguay

The UNODC estimate for cannabis

production in Paraguay was raised from 2,000 to slightly less than 6,000 metric tons, a threefold increase. However, the growth reported from Paraguay was even more dramatic, suggesting an annual production of some 15,000 metric tons of cannabis. The upsurge was explained by an increase in the cultivation area and the introduction of new species which allow for cannabis cultivation in the dry winter months, thus leading to higher yields.

However, the reported estimate did not tally with credible information that 85 per cent of Paraguayan cannabis resin (equivalent to 12,750 metric tons) is destined for cannabis markets in Brazil. Given the official estimates of cannabis users in Brazil (1 per cent of the population age 15-64 or 1.2 million persons), each user would have had to consume 10.5 kg of cannabis per year which is far in excess of the usual figures for annual use (100-250 grams per user). Absorption capacity in other South American countries is limited and no information has emerged so far from Paraguay conquering markets outside South America.

Therefore, taking all these factors into consideration, the estimate for cannabis production in Paraguay was raised more conservatively.

### Production also on the rise in Africa and Asia

Other major producing countries of cannabis herb are – according to UNODC estimates – Morocco (3,700 metric tons), South Africa (2,200 metric tons), Colombia (2,000 metric tons) and Nigeria (2,000 metric tons). Further important producer countries are:

Kazakhstan, Philippines, Egypt, Lebanon, Canada, India, Sri Lanka, Kyrgyzstan, Afghanistan, Albania

and Netherlands, with an estimated production ranging between 300 and 1,600 metric tons per country.

In Africa, cannabis production shows an upward trend, except for Morocco where production has declined sharply. A number of Asian countries also reported higher production estimates.

Although the changes at the global level have not been dramatic over the past two years, current production estimates are substantially higher than those for the early 1990s. After having fallen in the late 1980s, global cannabis production seems to be now more than twice as high as a decade earlier. The trend in production is in line with seizure data.

### Notes

1 This would be equivalent to either the new estimate of 3,000 hectares and the old yield of 1960 kg/ha or the old area under cultivation estimate (1,100 ha) and the new yield estimates of more than 5,000 kg/ha per year.

2 The estimate of cannabis herb production of Morocco was established on the basis of the cannabis cultivation survey carried out by the Government of Morocco, in collaboration with UNODC, and seizure data providing an indication of the likely split of cannabis resin and cannabis herb production. Taking the typical cannabis-to-cannabis-resin transformation ratios into account, seizure data suggest that less than 5 per cent of the land under cannabis cultivation in Morocco is dedicated to cannabis herb production. Based on these ratios, the total area under cannabis herb cultivation was estimated at 4,500 hectares in 2004. Using the average yield in Morocco (813 kg in 2004) resulted in an estimate of 3,660 metric tons of cannabis herb production in Morocco.

⇨ The above information is an extract from the United Nations Office on Drugs and Crime's *2006 World Drug Report* and is reprinted with permission. Visit www.unodc.org
© UNODC

# International cannabis statistics

## Statistics taken from the United Nations Office on Drugs and Crime's *2006 World Drug Report*

### Seizures of cannabis herb in kg – highest ranking countries, 2004

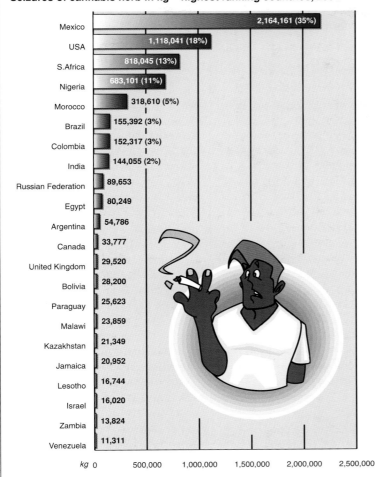

| Country | kg |
|---|---|
| Mexico | 2,164,161 (35%) |
| USA | 1,118,041 (18%) |
| S.Africa | 818,045 (13%) |
| Nigeria | 683,101 (11%) |
| Morocco | 318,610 (5%) |
| Brazil | 155,392 (3%) |
| Colombia | 152,317 (3%) |
| India | 144,055 (2%) |
| Russian Federation | 89,653 |
| Egypt | 80,249 |
| Argentina | 54,786 |
| Canada | 33,777 |
| United Kingdom | 29,520 |
| Bolivia | 28,200 |
| Paraguay | 25,623 |
| Malawi | 23,859 |
| Kazakhstan | 21,349 |
| Jamaica | 20,952 |
| Lesotho | 16,744 |
| Israel | 16,020 |
| Zambia | 13,824 |
| Venezuela | 11,311 |

kg  0    500,000    1,000,000    1,500,000    2,000,000    2,500,000

### Global cannabis market – breakdown by region

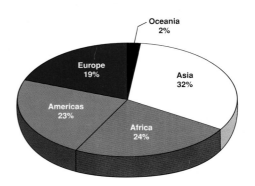

Oceania 2%
Europe 19%
Asia 32%
Americas 23%
Africa 24%

*Sources: UNODC Annual Reports Questionnaire Data, Govt. reports, reports of regional bodies, UNODC estimates.*

### Distribution of cannabis herb production in 2004/05 (N = 45,000 metric tons)

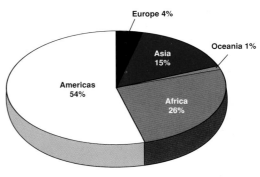

Europe 4%
Asia 15%
Oceania 1%
Americas 54%
Africa 26%

*Source: UNODC Annual Reports Questionnaire Data/DELTA*

### Annual prevalence of cannabis use, 2003-2005, in percentage of population age 15-64

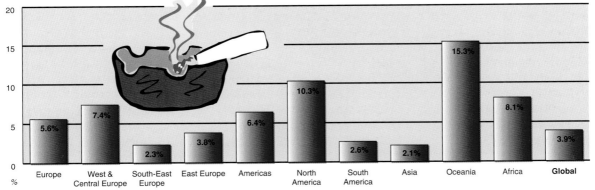

| Region | % |
|---|---|
| Europe | 5.6% |
| West & Central Europe | 7.4% |
| South-East Europe | 2.3% |
| East Europe | 3.8% |
| Americas | 6.4% |
| North America | 10.3% |
| South America | 2.6% |
| Asia | 2.1% |
| Oceania | 15.3% |
| Africa | 8.1% |
| Global | 3.9% |

*Sources: Annual Reports Questionnaire Data, various Government reports, reports of regional bodies, UNODC estimates.*

### Countries and sub-regions most frequently cited as sources of cannabis resin, 2002-2004 (based on data from 64 countries)*

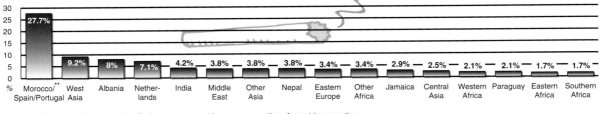

| Source | % |
|---|---|
| Morocco**/Spain/Portugal | 27.7% |
| West Asia | 9.2% |
| Albania | 8% |
| Netherlands | 7.1% |
| India | 4.2% |
| Middle East | 3.8% |
| Other Asia | 3.8% |
| Nepal | 3.8% |
| Eastern Europe | 3.4% |
| Other Africa | 3.4% |
| Jamaica | 2.9% |
| Central Asia | 2.5% |
| Western Africa | 2.1% |
| Paraguay | 2.1% |
| Eastern Africa | 1.7% |
| Southern Africa | 1.7% |

*\* number of times countries were identified as source countries, as a proportion of countries reporting.*
*\*\* shown together as they lie along the same trafficking route.*

*Source: UNODC, Annual Reports Questionnaire Data*

# Drug laws and licensing

## Frequently asked questions on the reclassification of cannabis

### Why has the Government reclassified cannabis?

The Advisory Council on the Misuse of Drugs advised that cannabis is harmful, but not as harmful as other Class B drugs, such as the amphetamines.

Reclassification brings the law into line with this assessment, and enables the Government to give a more credible message to young people about the relative dangers of drugs.

The change will help the Government to focus more effectively on Class A drugs – hard drugs such as heroin and crack/cocaine which cause the most harm – and on getting people into treatment.

### What is the legal effect of reclassification?

Cannabis, as a Class C drug, remains controlled under the Misuse of Drugs Act; and possessing it remains a criminal offence, but the maximum penalties for possession are reduced from five years' to two years' imprisonment. Maximum penalties for supplying and dealing in cannabis stay at 14 years' imprisonment.

### What laws have changed in connection with the reclassification of cannabis?

There are two changes:
⇨ Retaining the power of arrest for cannabis possession offences (under guidance issued by the police, there is a presumption against this power being used, unless there are specific aggravating factors).
⇨ Increasing the maximum penalty for supply and dealing in Class C drugs from five years' to 14 years' imprisonment. This means

that, on reclassification, the maximum penalty for trafficking cannabis remained at 14 years' imprisonment, and the courts continue to be able to impose substantial sentences for serious dealing offences.

### Does the reclassification of cannabis encourage greater use?

The law covers production so it applies to the sale and importation of kits.

There is no reason why it should. It remains an illegal drug and criminal sanctions continue to apply. In particular, the Government is taking a tough line with dealers. It backed up reclassification with an education campaign aimed at young people, to make it clear how the law operates in practice and to dissuade them from experimenting with cannabis.

The Advisory Council report on cannabis indicated that: 'In attempting to analyse the likely impact on prevalence of reclassification, there is very little relevant domestic learning to draw on. But it is possible to look at the experience of other countries, albeit in circumstances where civil penalties have replaced criminal sanctions. In particular, the experiences in Australia, the Netherlands and the United States

are illustrative. In each of these countries a reduction in the penalties for using cannabis has not led to a significant increase in use.'

### Why are drugs classified A, B or C?

The Misuse of Drugs Act 1971 places drugs into one of three categories, A, B or C, for the purposes of control. Classification broadly reflects the risks and harms caused by misuse of the controlled drug in question, and is reflected in penalty levels for drugs offences.

### What is the Advisory Council on the Misuse of Drugs?

This is the statutory, independent Government advisory body tasked to keep drug misuse and the legislation under review, and to advise the Government on the need for any changes.

The membership of this group comprises experience and expertise in a range of disciplines related to drug misuse.

### How is a drug reclassified?

An Order in Council is needed to move cannabis from the list of Class B drugs to Class C. The Order in Council is debated in, and has to be approved by, the Commons and Lords and has to be approved by the Privy Council.

### What do UN Conventions require?

The United Kingdom is signatory to three UN conventions on international co-operation in the drugs field. These require contracting states to establish as criminal offences the possession, production or cultivation of many drugs, including cannabis, for personal consumption.

*What is the date of reclassification?*
29th January 2004.

*What happens to someone who is found in possession of cannabis?*
Under the guidance being issued by the Association of Chief Police Officers (ACPO) to all police forces, there is a presumption against arrest. For adults, most offences of cannabis possession are likely to result in a warning and confiscation of the drug. But the following instances may lead to arrest and possible caution or prosecution:
⇨ repeat offending
⇨ smoking in a public place
⇨ instances where public order is threatened
⇨ possession of cannabis in the vicinity of premises used by children.
This is operational from the date of reclassification, 29th January 2004.

*By retaining the power of arrest, aren't you just maintaining the status quo?*
There is a presumption against arrest under the police guidance – previously there was no such presumption. In addition, following reclassification, the maximum penalty for the possession of cannabis went down from five years' to two years' imprisonment.

Reclassification sends a more credible message to young people that all drugs are harmful, but some are more harmful than others.

*How are young people under 18 being dealt with?*
The Government is sending out a clear message to young people under 18 that cannabis use remains illegal.
Police enforcement is consistent with the more structured framework for early juvenile offending established under the Crime and Disorder Act 1998, where a young offender can receive a reprimand, final warning or charge depending on the seriousness of the offence. Following one reprimand, any further offence will lead to a final warning or charge.
Any further offence following a warning will normally result in a charge being brought. After a final warning, the young offender must be referred to the Youth Offending Team to arrange a rehabilitation programme to prevent reoffending.

*Why are young people being dealt with more strictly than adults?*
They are not being dealt with more strictly – they are likely to receive reprimands or warnings for a first offence of cannabis possession. However, the process is more formal for persons under 18, and it is important that their cases should be dealt with at the police station, so that any underlying problems with the young person can be identified.
Young people under the age of 18 who receive a final warning, or are reported for court proceedings for the possession of cannabis, will be referred to the local Youth Offending Team (YOT), and are likely to have their substance misuse assessed by the YOT drugs worker, who may arrange treatment or other support where this is needed.

*Does reclassification mean people are able to smoke openly?*
No. Those who smoke openly in public face possible arrest and prosecution.

---

**Reclassification sends a more credible message to young people that all drugs are harmful, but some are more harmful than others**

---

*How can you ensure that the police enforce the law in a consistent way and don't overuse the power of arrest?*
The Association of Chief Police Officers (ACPO) is committed to the guidance, and to ensuring that it is operated consistently and within its spirit.
ACPO keeps operation of the guidance under constant review. In addition, HM Chief Inspector of Constabulary closely monitors the guidance's use, and will intervene with any police force where necessary.

*What action are you taking against those people who intend to set up cannabis cafés?*
Anyone trying to establish a cannabis café risks imprisonment or a heavy fine (or both). Supply of cannabis remains a criminal offence, and those who sell it to others risk severe penalties. It is also an offence for managers of premises to allow smoking or supply of cannabis on their premises.

YOU HAVE BEEN WARNED. HAVE A NICE DAY!

Reclassification of cannabis makes no difference to this position. We expect the police to respond swiftly and effectively to any such attempts to defy the law. Smoking cannabis in a cannabis café (or elsewhere) could result in arrest and prosecution.

### Why are we not adopting the Dutch model?

In Holland, the small-scale possession and supply of cannabis remain illegal but there is a formal policy of tolerance of small-scale selling and possession of cannabis in coffee shops. But coffee shops still have to go to the criminal markets for their supplies.

Dutch experience also shows us how difficult it is to restrict the sale of cannabis, including to children, through a licensed source.

### What are the harmful effects of cannabis?

The acute effects include damage to people's ability to learn and carry out many tasks, including operating machinery and driving vehicles. Acute cannabis intoxication can also lead to panic attacks, paranoia and confused feelings.

The chronic effects include damage to mental functioning and in particular to learning difficulties, which in prolonged and heavy users may not necessarily be reversible. A cannabis dependence syndrome has been identified in heavy users and the drug can exacerbate schizophrenia in people who are already affected. Smoking cannabis over a long period of time can lead to respiratory diseases, including lung cancer.

### What about reports that cannabis smoking leads to lung cancer?

Smoking cannabis presents a real health risk, potentially similar to that of tobacco. Smoked cannabis has a higher concentration of certain carcinogens than smoked tobacco, and it tends to be inhaled more deeply.

However, in general cannabis smokers smoke fewer cigarettes per day than tobacco smokers and most give up in their 30s. A Department of Health working group is examining the health consequences of cannabis smoking.

## Drug classifications

**Classification of illegal drugs**

| Classification | Drugs | Maximum penalties |
|---|---|---|
| Class A | Heroin, LSD, ecstasy, amphetamines (prepared for injection), cocaine and crack cocaine, magic mushrooms | For posession: 7 years' imprisonment and/or fine. For supply: life imprisonment and/or fine. |
| Class B | Amphetamines, methylamphetamine, barbiturates, codeine | For posession: 5 years' imprisonment and/or fine. For supply: 14 years' imprisonment and/or fine. |
| Class C | Cannabis, temazepam, anabolic steroids, valium, ketamine, methylphenidate (Ritalin), gamma-hydroxy butyrate (GHB) | For posession: 2 years' imprisonment and/or fine. For supply: 14 years' imprisonment and/or fine. |

Source: From Drug classification: making a hash of it, a report of the Science and Technology Committee ordered by the House of Commons. Published 31 July 2006. Crown copyright.

### Is cannabis a 'gateway' drug leading to use of more harmful drugs? / Won't this lead to more people taking hard drugs?

The evidence for cannabis as a 'gateway' drug, which leads on to other drug use, is inconclusive. Research confirms that establishing a causal link is extremely difficult. It is clear that most users of the more dangerous drugs used cannabis earlier in their careers, but most cannabis users do not go on to use other drugs regularly.

---

## Smoked cannabis has a higher concentration of certain carcinogens than smoked tobacco, and it tends to be inhaled more deeply

---

Of course, the same can be said of alcohol. Very large numbers of those who use Class A drugs have used alcohol to excess. But many people who use alcohol do not progress to any form of other drug.

### What are you doing to educate young people about the dangers of cannabis?

To coincide with reclassification, the Government issued a fact sheet which is widely available to young people, which explains that cannabis remains illegal and describes what will happen to someone who is found in possession of cannabis. The 3-year national campaign – FRANK – to alert young people to the harm of all drugs includes information about cannabis.

### Will the Government permit the use of cannabis for medicinal purposes?

The Home Secretary is willing to amend the misuse of drugs legislation as necessary, to allow the prescribing of a cannabis-based medicine as a form of pain relief. The Home Office granted a licence to GW Pharmaceuticals who have conducted trials and have developed a cannabis-based medicine designed to relieve chronic nerve pain.

The company has been seeking marketing approval for the product from the Medicines and Healthcare products Regulatory Agency (MHRA) – a process all new medicines have to go through which is designed to protect public health. In November 2004, the Committee for the Safety of Medicines advised the MHRA not to grant a licence without further tests. This decision is open to appeal.

⇨ The above information is reprinted with kind permission from the Home Office. Visit www.drugs.gov.uk for more information.

© Crown copyright

# Kate's story

## Cannabis and her son

Scrawled in thick black pen and pinned to my son's bedroom wall were the words: 'I don't want to feel like this – make it stop.'

I took my once lively teenage son Guy to the GP. A week later, he saw a psychiatrist. I waited nervously outside. When he called me in, nothing could have prepared me for his words:

'Guy is displaying psychotic behaviour, brought on, in all probability, from smoking cannabis.'

I was shocked. Alarm bells rang in my head – my son was a junkie. How had we, as parents, allowed this to happen? I couldn't believe a supposedly harmless drug had done this to my son.

But as we were to find out, the damage was already done. Guy withdrew completely and two weeks later he overdosed. He was admitted to a Mental Health Unit. Every day I visited him and he would often talk to the air.

'It's the voices,' he said, tapping his temple. My blood ran cold.

After two months, Guy was discharged. He tried to lead a normal life. The thought of mixing with people frightened him and some days he would not leave his bedroom.

I was constantly on stand-by in case something happened. The son I had nurtured was gone; there was a shadow in his place.

Guy took himself off the tablets and was signed off psychiatric care. Six months later, thinking he was on the mend, Guy smoked a joint. It sent him spiralling into another depression.

The doctors advised us that he would need lengthy treatment. One day, after his doctor's appointment, I dropped him at home, but I couldn't rest easy. Something was telling me to go back. The house was eerily silent. I called Guy's name.

Guy had hanged himself from the bed frame with a scarf.

His face was pale and his eyes bulged. Guy was brain dead by the time he reached the hospital. The only thing keeping him alive was a ventilator. The next day, my husband and I made the heartbreaking decision to turn the machine off. An hour later, he slipped peacefully away.

At home, lying on his unmade bed was his black beanie hat and a rejection letter from a job application.

Now, a year on, I want to warn other mothers about cannabis and its links to mental illness. I'm starting my own awareness campaign by sharing Guy's story.

What happened to him won't happen to everyone who smokes a joint, but people need to be aware of the risks.

⇨ The above information is reprinted with kind permission from FRANK. Visit www.talktofrank.com for more information.

© FRANK

# Common misconceptions about reclassification

## Information from UKCIA

Due to the somewhat ambiguous and confusing language used by the Government to define reclassification, and the sometimes downright wrong way that some of the mass media has reported it, there are several common misconceptions that people hold about what reclassification means for them. Some of these are that:

*Cannabis is legal to use.* **Wrong** – cannabis use is still 100% illegal. It will still be a criminal offence to possess cannabis, with a punishment of possible jail term. However, if caught with a small amount of cannabis the police are expected to not 'fully' arrest you unless there are 'aggravated' circumstances in their opinion, but they will confiscate it and take your details.

*Cannabis has been decriminalised.* **Wrong** – it is still a criminal offence under the Misuse of Drugs Act, and even simple possession carries a risk of gaining a criminal record.

*You are allowed to use cannabis in your own home.* **Wrong** – whilst the police are unlikely to specifically pursue you for such behaviour alone, if they catch you they will still confiscate it and take your details. They can still fully arrest you if they so wish, particularly if there are aggravating circumstances. Nothing has changed in the supply laws, so technically passing a spliff or bong to your friends is still a supply offence, punishable by anything up to 14 years. However, this level of punishment is highly unlikely, just as it was before.

*This is the first step on the road to legalisation.* **Wrong** – the Government have made it clear that they have no intentions to legalise or decriminalise cannabis. There are no plans to further change the status of cannabis after its reclassification.

⇨ The above information is reprinted with kind permission from the UK Cannabis Internet Activists. Visit www.ukcia.org for more information.

© UKCIA

# Why drug laws damage cannabis users' health

## Information from the Lifeline Project

When cannabis was reclassified from a Class B to a Class C drug in Britain in January 2004, it seemed like a fairly liberal change which would reduce legal harm to cannabis users (criminalisation, imprisonment, etc.). However, at the same time, so as not to give a signal that they were going soft on drug dealers, the government raised the penalties for trafficking Class C drugs to those of Class B levels. Thus, though the maximum prison sentence for possessing cannabis dropped from five to two years, the maximum prison sentence for trafficking cannabis (production, intent to supply, supply, import/export, etc.) remained 14 years.

This change has resulted in an increase in overall harm – that is, cannabis users now face greater harm to their health, as well as the same level of legal harm for any offence other than possession. How exactly does the revised law increase health risks to cannabis users? Let's start at the beginning.

### Smoking formula

Atha's research (Independent Drug Monitoring Unit 2004) shows that cannabis resin comprises about half of the UK cannabis market, and skunk (herbal cannabis grown with artificial lights, hydroponics, etc.) comprises most of the rest. The main form of cannabis resin product in the UK is 'formula' – typically Moroccan soap-bar cannabis – a low grade product heavily adulterated with various toxic and unhygienic substances, from engine oil and vinyl to soil and animal excrement (e.g. CRISP 2001). Based on the British Crime Survey findings and Atha's research, it can be estimated that about two to three million people primarily smoke (or eat) formula,

which is typically purchased in tenths, eighths or quarters (about 2-7 grams) off dealers. If they are caught in possession of 'personal' amounts by the police (how much varies by force area, but it usually covers at least three grams), all that happens is that they will be given a warning, the drug will be confiscated, and their name and address will be taken. This can happen up to three times a year – after that (or if there are aggravating circumstances like using in public), they may be cautioned, or eventually even prosecuted (when they would probably be fined, rather than face the maximum two-year prison sentence). Of course, the price formula users pay for this relative freedom from prosecution is greater risks to their physical health from the toxic muck they are smoking.

### Smoking and growing skunk

Should a cannabis user choose to avoid the health-damaging consequences of using formula by using the main available alternative (skunk), they are likely to find that the demand well outstrips the erratic supply (a mixture of Dutch imports and British home-grown skunk). Even when it can be obtained, the cost (£40-50 a quarter) is up to three times that of a quarter of formula. So, given the cost and other hassles of commercial skunk, many users turn to growing their own herbal cannabis. Of course, the only realistic option in Britain (because of the poor sunlight and weather) is to grow cannabis indoors under artificial lights. Growers start with seeds or cuttings, and can grow in soil, or just with water and nutrients (hydroponics). Since a typical growth cycle is three months, and since one standard 400-watt sodium light can grow about four plants, the minimum number of plants grown by most cultivators is about four (producing a typical dry yield of about two to four ounces of bud, i.e. about half-ounce to one ounce per plant). Given that

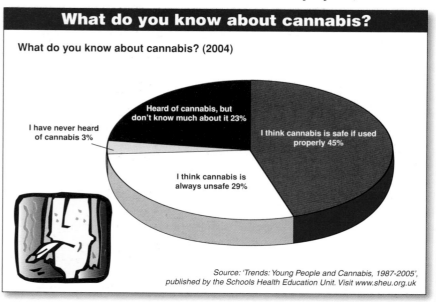

**What do you know about cannabis?**

What do you know about cannabis? (2004)

- Heard of cannabis, but don't know much about it 23%
- I have never heard of cannabis 3%
- I think cannabis is safe if used properly 45%
- I think cannabis is always unsafe 29%

*Source: 'Trends: Young People and Cannabis, 1987-2005', published by the Schools Health Education Unit. Visit www.sheu.org.uk*

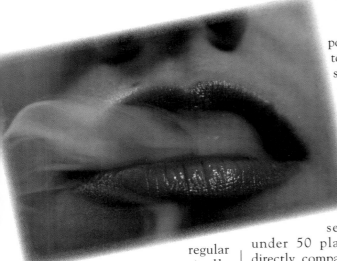

regular users typically consume about one ounce per month (up to two ounces for heavier users), this would be enough for about two to four months for a moderate user, or one or two months for a heavier user (or a couple of moderate users). Of course, someone who wished to grow enough cannabis for six to 12 months would grow at least 12 plants. This would require about three sodium lamps, and could be done in a large cupboard – clearly a small-scale endeavour rather than a commercial operation.

## Penalties for possession and production

Do people convicted of cannabis production get bigger sentences than people convicted of cannabis possession? Though official statistics do not permit a direct assessment of this question, the available figures are consistent with the general hypothesis that the courts regard growing cannabis as more criminal than simply possessing it.

Statistics on cannabis seized by the police in the UK generally lump together seizures of all sizes (i.e. from both possession and supply cases), and so figures for average amounts seized are at least ten times higher than the amounts typically involved in a case of simple possession. In 2002, the mean amount of herbal cannabis seized was 103 grams, compared with 182 grams for cannabis resin. Even so, about 70% of herbal cannabis seizures involved amounts under one gram, as did 47% of cannabis resin seizures; and 99% of seizures of both types of cannabis were under 500 grams. Of course, people caught with more than about 10-30 grams of cannabis are usually charged with

possession with intent to supply, rather than simple possession – a practice which became law under the 2005 Drugs Act. Turning to cannabis plants, the mean number seized in 2002 was 23, with 91% of all plant seizures involving under 50 plants. Though not directly comparable, these figures are consistent with the hypothesis that the majority of cases of both cannabis possession and production involved amounts consistent with personal use.

Yet average sentences for cannabis production have been notably stiffer than those for cannabis possession throughout the 2000s. For instance, in 2000, there were 75,986 cannabis offenders, including 70,306 (93%) for possession, and 1,960 (3%) for production. There were three salient differences in sentencing for these two types of offence. First, almost half (48%) of possession cases received a police caution, compared with less than a quarter (23%) of production cases. Second, 6% of possession cases received some kind of probation supervision, compared with 19% of production cases. Third, as well as being three times more likely to receive probation, production offenders were also four times more likely than possession offenders to receive an unsuspended prison sentence (12% compared with 3%). Furthermore, among cannabis offenders sentenced to imprisonment, sentence lengths were four to five times higher for production offenders compared with possession offenders. For example, between 2000 and 2002, sentence lengths averaged 3-4 months for possession, but ranged between 12 and 17 months for production (a similar difference was found for average fines – e.g., in 2002, £84 for possession and £132 for production).

## Why growing cannabis is more criminal than buying it

National and local newspapers regularly report prison sentences of

6-12 months (sometimes higher) being handed out to people caught growing 10 to 20 plants, or even as few as five. The reasons for such high sentences appear to be:

1 the offence is classified as trafficking (production) rather than possession for personal use (it used to be called cultivation, but was bundled under production about a decade ago);

2 the product is of relatively high THC purity (8-16% compared with 3%-8% for cannabis resin);

3 it involves technical equipment and procedures (the equipment and plants can be made to look like evidence of a large-scale criminal operation when exhibited out of context in a courtroom); and

4 small-scale indoor cultivation typically produces a yield of around two to 12 ounces – and this is usually seen by the police and courts as an amount consistent with an intention to supply, rather than an amount indicative of personal use over several months. Yet a wine-maker who stored a year's supply of wine in their cellar would be unlikely to be viewed as an unlicensed alcohol supplier.

And this brings us to the question we started with: how does cannabis reclassification increase health harm to cannabis users? Answer: in order to reduce the risk of imprisonment associated with growing cannabis, British cannabis users have to buy off drug dealers, which means (1) purchasing and consuming the most adulterated and toxic form of the drug (formula), and thus (2) risking damage to their health; as well as (3) having regular contact with drug dealers who may sell other drugs; and also (4) paying high prices for low-grade cannabis, rather than lower costs for better quality home-grown. This is the result of the drug laws. By prohibiting cannabis, the government did not end supply, but simply abdicated responsibility for supply to criminal gangs – who, operating in an unregulated market for maximum profits, inevitably adulterate their drug products. Unfortunately, because cannabis resin is such an unusual (difficult) substance to simulate (smell, colour, texture, etc.), all sorts of toxic substances end up in the 'mix'.

Our cannabis laws have always been unjustified and counter-productive, but they have now become downright stupid – and human stupidity has always been one of the greatest causes of unnecessary harm. I have spent many years thinking about and debating our drug laws, yet I still find it hard to believe that the police can actually burst into someone's house and arrest them for growing a bunch of innocuous plants, or possessing their dried leaves and flowers. That such victims of our drug laws can then be prosecuted and possibly imprisoned for several months/years is almost unbelievable. It never ceases to amaze me how political paternalism (the nanny state) and public ignorance/apathy can combine to lead to the passing of laws about which flowers you can grow or have – in a democratic country!

---

**The available figures are consistent with the general hypothesis that the courts regard growing cannabis as more criminal than simply possessing it**

### Conclusion

To conclude, just think about some of the things you can do to hurt yourself which are legal (as long as you are of sound mind):

1 you can buy and smoke the most dangerous drug known to humankind, which kills up to half of its users – tobacco – or take our other legal drug in amounts which can rot your liver and damage your brain (millions of Brits booze past the safe limits every day);

2 you can grow and consume almost all but a small number of plants and fungi, including highly poisonous species such as deadly nightshade, poison ivy and death cap mushrooms;

3 you can get your kicks by participating in leisure activities which carry a high risk of serious injury

or death – such as mountain climbing and bungee jumping;

4 you can mutilate and inflict terrible pain on yourself, if that turns you on (yes, masochism is legal too);

5 and, since 1963 in Britain, you can even kill yourself (though not so long ago, failed suicides faced the death penalty!).

We live in a country where you can legally maim or kill yourself in many ways, but in which you can be imprisoned for growing or having a relatively harmless flower. We really do.

*'There is no better rough test of a soul than its attitude to drugs'*
Aleister Crowley (1922). Diary of a Drug Fiend.
*Dr Russell Newcombe, Senior Lecturer in Drug Use & Addiction, Liverpool John Moores University, Liverpool, England*
*April 2005*

⇨ The above information is reprinted with kind permission from Lifeline Project. Visit www.lifeline.org.uk for more information on this topic.

© *Lifeline*

# Cannabis users with just 10 joints face 14 years' jail

## By Philip Johnston

**D**rug users caught in possession of enough cannabis for just 10 joints could be classified as dealers and face up to 14 years in jail under proposals being considered in Whitehall.

The Home Office is looking at new thresholds on the amount of illegal substances classified as merely possession rather than intent to supply.

There was an outcry last year when the Home Office proposed that cannabis smokers should be allowed to have enough of the drug to make more than 500 joints and still claim it was for personal use. This appeared to reinforce the more 'softly, softly' approach to cannabis possession that was behind the decision to re-categorise the drug from a Class B to a Class C drug.

But the Home Office has now performed what one MP yesterday called a 'dramatic flip-flop' and is proposing far smaller thresholds which campaigners said could end up sending casual users to prison as dealers.

The Home Office has written to the Government's experts, the Advisory Committee on the Misuse of Drugs, telling them that ministers are minded to set the threshold for cannabis possession at just 5g – enough to make between 10 and 20 joints – compared with the 500g first proposed.

For ecstasy the limit would be five pills against 10 in the earlier plans while the limit for amphetamines would be 14g in line with the original proposal. Possession of cocaine, heroin or crack cocaine would be just two grammes against the seven proposed.

The documents also showed that the Government's official advisors on drug policy, the Advisory Council on the Misuse of Drugs, favoured a higher 10g limit for cannabis possession.

Nick Clegg, the Liberal Democrat home affairs spokesman, said: 'This dramatic shift in policy shows the Government is in a state of total panic and chaos.'

He added: 'Labour's flip-flopping is simply not an adequate response.'

David Davis, the shadow home secretary, said: 'This is a move in a sensible direction, but continuous changes by the Government have only added to the confusion.'
*8 June 2006*

© *Telegraph Group Limited 2006*

# Cannabis: why we should care

## Information taken from the *2006 World Drug Report*

The global community is confused about cannabis. On the one hand, cannabis is controlled with the same degree of severity as heroin and cocaine under the Single Convention on Narcotic Drugs, 1961. Virtually every country in the world is a party to that Convention. On the other hand, however, cannabis offences are treated far more leniently than those related to other narcotic drugs in many countries. A conflicting message is thus sent to the population and it is no wonder that public opinion becomes confused.

Rather than confronting this schism head-on, cannabis has been allowed to fall into a grey area. Technically illegal but widely de-prioritised, the drug has grown in popularity at a rate outpacing all others while simultaneously enriching those willing to break the law. A global blind-spot has developed around cannabis, and in this murk the plant itself has been transformed into something far more potent than in the past. Suddenly, the mental health impact of cannabis use has been thrown into sharp relief, and the drug with which the world has felt so familiar seems strange once again.

Coming to terms with cannabis is important because it is, by quite a wide margin, the world's most popular illicit drug. An estimated 4 per cent of the world's adult population consumes it each year, more than all the other illicit drugs combined. In some countries, more than half of the young people polled have tried it. Mankind has cultivated the plant for a variety of reasons for centuries, and it has been the subject of reams of academic research in the last 50 years alone, including recent studies of its therapeutic applications.

Given this wealth of knowledge and experience, it is rather surprising that many basic facts about the drug remain unknown. Concerned with the situation, Member States requested UNODC, in General Assembly resolution 59/160, to prepare a global market survey on cannabis. However, when it comes to the mechanics of the market, the world's biggest illicit drug is actually the least understood. In contrast to drug crops like coca and opium poppy, very little is known about the extent of cannabis cultivation around the world. In fact, few Governments can confidently give an estimate of the scale of cultivation in their own countries. In the United States, for example, a country with both resources and a strong infrastructure for drug control, official estimates of the extent of domestic cultivation vary by more than a factor of six. Even if the number of hectares under cannabis were documented, there has been little study of how much drug product these fields would yield. As a result, global production estimates remain highly tentative.

There are several reasons why these questions are so difficult to answer. Unlike other drug crops, cannabis can be grown virtually anywhere, including indoors, and there are very few countries where it can be definitively said that cannabis is not cultivated. Moreover, cannabis is both easy to grow and highly productive, yielding a large quantity of ready-to-use drug per plant. As a result, many users can, and do, produce their own supply. Current illicit crop monitoring techniques, such as satellite surveillance, are of little use in assessing cultivation taking place in private homes and small plots in communities spread across the globe. In addition, there remain unanswered questions about

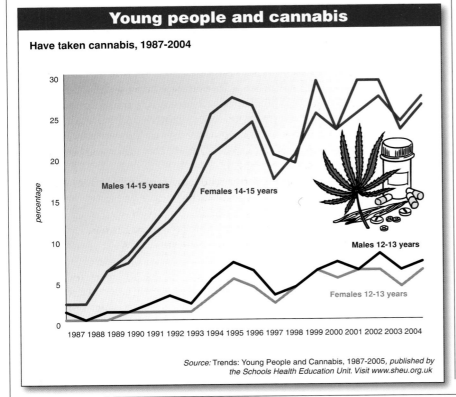

**Young people and cannabis**

**Have taken cannabis, 1987-2004**

Males 14-15 years

Females 14-15 years

Males 12-13 years

Females 12-13 years

*percentage*

30
25
20
15
10
5
0

1987 1988 1989 1990 1991 1992 1993 1994 1995 1996 1997 1998 1999 2000 2001 2002 2003 2004

*Source:* Trends: Young People and Cannabis, 1987-2005, *published by the Schools Health Education Unit. Visit www.sheu.org.uk*

basic aspects of cannabis use, such as the precise amounts bought and consumed by users.

Many of these issues could be cleared up with appropriate targeted research. The fact that this research has not been done reflects the global ambiguity on cannabis. These political attitudes reflect popular perceptions that cannabis is different from other controlled substances. Indeed, many of the risks associated with other illicit drugs are not an issue with cannabis. It is nearly impossible to die of an overdose of cannabis. Because it is relatively cheap in most markets, crimes associated with acquiring money for cannabis dependency are limited. In many parts of the developed world, cannabis is regarded as a soporific, and the behaviour of the intoxicated as humorous, not dangerous. For many, it is a point of faith that cannabis is harmless, the victim of relentless disinformation.

It is true that much of the early material on cannabis is now considered inaccurate, and that a series of studies in a range of countries have exonerated cannabis of many of the charges levelled against it. But the latest research indicates that the pendulum may have swung too far in the opposite direction. There are serious mental health consequences associated with cannabis, including a significant risk of dependency, precipitation and aggravation of psychosis, and acute dysphoric episodes. These risks appear to be higher for people who start consuming cannabis during adolescence. Each year, thousands of people seek medical attention for problems related to their cannabis use, and this number appears to be growing. Cannabis is not the harmless herb often portrayed, but a psychoactive drug that deserves to be taken seriously.

One reason these serious effects are only being appreciated now is that they appear to be related to the growth of high-potency cannabis in many countries where such research is commonly done. For the last several decades, cannabis breeders and cultivation experts have laboured to transform the plant, creating a much more potent and productive version of the drug previously reviewed. These developments were reviewed, along with other aspects of the cannabis market, in a double issue of the *Bulletin on Narcotics* (Volume XLIX, Nos.1 and 2, 1997; Volume L, Nos.1 and 2, 1998). The situation has advanced considerably since that time. High-potency cannabis may be responsible for the growing number of people seeking help for cannabis problems in developed countries around the world. Although most of the cannabis consumed globally is grown the traditional way, the problems associated with the 'new' cannabis may simply be large-print versions of issues not recognised before.

⇨ The above information is an extract from the United Nations Office on Drugs and Crime's *2006 World Drug Report* and is reprinted with permission. Visit www.unodc.org for more information.

© UNODC

# Cannabis: the science

**Cannabis is also known as marijuana, draw, blow, weed, puff, shit, hash, ganja, spliff, brown, dope, gear, green, pot and solids. It can be eaten or rolled with (or without) tobacco into a cigarette and smoked**

## From

Cannabis is a natural substance from a plant commonly called hemp (*cannabis sativa*). The plant can be found growing wild all over the world and it is easily cultivated in the UK. It contains chemicals called cannabinoids, including delta-9-tetrahydrocannabinol (THC), which is believed to be responsible for most of the drug's psychoactive effects. The first recorded use of cannabis was in 2700 BC as a medicine in China. The first archaeological remains of cannabis in England date back to 400 AD where evidence suggests that it was cultivated at Old Buckenham Mere. In 1563, under the rule of Queen Elizabeth I, it was law that if you owned more than 60 acres of land, some of it had to be set aside to grow cannabis, or you would be fined five pounds. Recreational use of cannabis was first prohibited in England in 1928.

## Chemistry

When users smoke cannabis the THC is absorbed into the blood stream, which takes it from the lungs to the heart and then the brain. THC mimics the actions of receptors in the brain called neurotransmitters and interferes with normal functions. It stimulates brain receptors in the frontal cortex, enabling users to experience heightened senses and a general feeling of relaxation. The cannabinoids in cannabis also block some of the electrical signals in the brain, interfering with the short-term memory and coordination of the users, while endo-cannabinoids bind with brain receptors to increase hunger (and bring on the munchies).

## Production

Cannabis is a tobacco-like substance produced by drying the leaves and flowering tops of the cannabis plant. As the unfertilised female flowers mature they continually secrete resin which coats the flowers and small leaves surrounding them. Hashish is produced when the resin is separated from the plant material while 'grass' is made from the dried and chopped leafy parts of the plant.

⇨ The above information is reprinted with kind permission from TheSite.org. Visit www.thesite.org for more information.

© TheSite.org

# Your rights on arrest

## Information from Release

You do not have to say anything to the police. But if you are later charged with a crime and you have not mentioned, when questioned, something that you later rely on in court, then this may be taken into account when deciding if you are guilty.

There may be good reason why you do not wish to say anything to the police, and you should not be intimidated into answering questions. Get a solicitor down to see you in the police station as soon as possible.

Remember:
⇒ There may be times when if you give an innocent explanation for what you have done, the police may leave you alone.
⇒ It is wise NOT to discuss the case with the police until you have consulted privately with a solicitor.
⇒ If the police are about to arrest you or have already arrested you, there is no such thing as a 'friendly chat' to sort things out. Anything you say can later be used against you. Think before you talk.

### When the police get it wrong

If you want to challenge anything the police have done, then get the names and addresses of any witnesses

**RELEASE**

and the name or number of the police officer/s, and make a written record as soon as possible after the incident. This should be witnessed, dated and signed. If you are injured, or property is damaged, then take photographs or video recordings as soon as possible and have physical injuries medically examined.

If you have been treated unfairly, then complain to the Independent Police Complaints Commission (www.ipcc.gov.uk), and contact a civil liberties group like Release or a Citizens' Advice Bureau or a solicitor about any possible legal action.

### On the street

If you are stopped by the police:
⇒ If they are not in uniform, then ask to see their warrant card.
⇒ Ask why you have been stopped and, at the end, ask for a record of the search.
⇒ You can be stopped and searched if the police have a reasonable suspicion that you are in possession of:

↳ controlled drugs
↳ offensive weapon or firearm
↳ carrying a sharp article
↳ carrying stolen goods
↳ or if you are in a coach or train, on your way to, or you have arrived at, a sports stadium.

There are other situations where you can be stopped and searched, for example:
⇒ If police fear that there might be serious violence or a terrorist threat in a particular area, they can stop and search anyone in that area for up to 48 hours. In these circumstances, the police do not need to have reasonable suspicion that you are carrying a weapon or committing a crime.

Remember:
⇒ You run the risk of both physical injury and serious criminal charges if you physically resist a search. If it is an unlawful search, you should take action afterwards by using the law.

### In the police station

You always have the right:
⇒ to be treated humanely and with respect.
⇒ to see the written Codes governing your rights and how you are to be treated.
⇒ to speak to the custody officer (the officer who MUST look after your welfare).
⇒ to know why you have been arrested.
⇒ to have present with you a responsible adult if you are 17 years or below.

You also have the right (but they can in rare situations be delayed):
⇒ to have someone notified of your arrest (not to make a phone call yourself).
⇒ to consult with a solicitor privately.
⇒ to request for a medical examiner to attend to you if you feel unwell.

Inform the custody officer at the earliest opportunity if you are on prescribed medication. You may in

"Just a friendly chat!"

certain circumstances be permitted to ingest, or negotiate for the collection and administration of, your medication. If not, notify your solicitor and refer him to PACE 1984 Code C Part 9.

Remember:

⇨ Do not panic. The police sometimes keep you isolated and waiting in the cell. Above all else, try to keep calm. The police can only keep you for a certain period of time – normally a maximum of 24 hours (36 hours for a serious arrestable offence, 48 hours for a terrorist offence). Further extensions of custody can be obtained in exceptional circumstances.

⇨ Make sure the correct time for your arrest is on your custody record.

⇨ Make sure you know why you have been arrested.

⇨ Insist on seeing a solicitor even though you might have to wait. Always request that a solicitor be present when you are interviewed. Do not be put off seeing a solicitor by the police. It is YOUR RIGHT, and it is FREE.

⇨ If you ask for anything and it is refused, make sure this is recorded in your custody record.

### Search of your home

⇨ The police can search premises with the consent of the occupier.

⇨ A warrant can be obtained from magistrates by the police to search premises for evidence of certain crimes.

⇨ The police can only search the section of the premises that you occupy and communal areas of the premises.

⇨ Police may enter WITHOUT a search warrant in many situations, including:

↳ following an arrest, the police are allowed to search premises the detained person occupies or has control over

↳ to capture an escaped prisoner

↳ to arrest a person for an arrestable offence or certain public order offences

↳ to protect life or to stop serious damage to property

↳ other laws give police specific powers to enter premises

Remember:

⇨ You are entitled to see a copy of any search warrant.

⇨ Police can use reasonable force to gain entry.

⇨ Police should give you information about their powers to search premises.

⇨ A record of the search must be kept by the police.

⇨ You or a friend should be allowed to be present during the search but this right can be refused if it is thought it might hinder investigations.

*This information is provided only as a brief guide to your rights on arrest – legal advice should always be sought if someone is in trouble with the police, or has a complaint against them.*

⇨ Release is the national centre of expertise on drugs, the law and human rights, providing free legal services to the socially excluded. Release relies on charitable donations to continue its work – please go to www.release.org.uk if you would like to make a contribution. Their helpline is on 0845 450 0215 and can be reached 11am to 1pm, Monday to Friday.

© Release

# Cannabis and cannabis extracts

## Information from the Multiple Sclerosis Society

People have claimed that cannabis, also known as 'marijuana', is an effective treatment for MS. Cannabis contains chemicals known as 'cannabinoids' including tetrahydrocannabinol (known as 'THC' for short). These cannabinoids have a variety of biological effects, and it is thought they may improve MS symptoms or affect how MS progresses. People who took part in a clinical trial suggested that cannabis, or cannabinoid preparations, may alleviate some symptoms, including spasticity and pain. Further studies of the effects of cannabis are planned in the UK.

Meanwhile, a cannabis-based drug called 'Sativex' is also now available in Canada, but does not have a licence in the UK. It can be prescribed by GPs on a 'named patient' basis, but this is the exception rather than the norm.

This creates a dilemma. Medically tested cannabis-based treatments, of known quality, are not available to most people in the UK. Some people therefore seek to find cannabis from other sources. However, currently cannabis is a class C controlled drug. Possession, production and supply of cannabis is illegal, and what is supplied illegally can vary wildly in nature and strength. The maximum penalty for possession of cannabis is two years' imprisonment. The Home Office advise that it is unlikely that adults caught in possession of cannabis will be arrested. Most offences of possession result in warning and confiscation of the drug. However, arrest, caution and prosecution may occur if someone repeatedly offends, smokes cannabis in a public place, or possesses cannabis in the vicinity of premises used by children.

Be aware that cannabis has many side effects including dizziness, sleepiness, feelings of intoxication, nausea, increased risk of seizures, poor pregnancy outcomes, and impaired driving. High doses of cannabis may decrease reaction time, impair heart function, and produce coordination and visual difficulties. Chronic use of cannabis may impair lung function, cause heart attacks, increase the risk of lung, mouth and throat cancer, and has been linked to psychological problems.

⇨ The above information is reprinted with kind permission from the Multiple Sclerosis Society. Visit www.mssociety.org.uk for more information.

© Multiple Sclerosis Society

# Medicinal cannabis and the law

**Prosecutors take a tough line on cannabis supplied to relieve pain**

⇨ *Up to 30% of MS sufferers estimated to use drug*
⇨ *Four linked to support groups face charges*

Prosecutors are taking a firm line on the supply of cannabis for pain relief to people with chronically painful conditions such as multiple sclerosis, despite the downgrading of the drug from class B to class C.

Two crown court trials, one starting this week and one next week, will accuse four individuals of supplying illegal drugs through the organisations Bud Buddies and THCforMS (Therapeutic Help from Cannabis for Multiple Sclerosis).

THCforMS says on its website that it has supplied 33,000 bars of cannabis chocolate to bona fide MS sufferers over the last five years. Mark Gibson, Lezley Gibson and Marcus Davies of THCforMS face a charge of conspiracy to supply cannabis in a trial that begins next Wednesday at Carlisle crown court.

Bud Buddies offered a number of cannabis preparations including cannabis cream for topical application to anyone with a proven medical need.

Its founder, Jeffrey Ditchfield, faces nine charges of cultivation and supply of cannabis, including a charge of supplying a cannabis plant received by John Reid, now home secretary, in November 2005. His trial starts on July 24 at Mold crown court. All four face maximum sentences of 14 years in prison.

Estimates suggest that between 10% and 30% of MS sufferers in Europe use cannabis to alleviate the pain and distressing symptoms of the disease.

Many say it alleviates their symptoms where ordinary

**By Clare Dyer, Legal Editor**

prescription drugs have failed. Few medicines are effective for treating MS, which affects around 85,000 people in the UK.

MS patients say the prosecutions, if successful, will close down this route to help, while the government drags its heels on licensing a cannabis-based drug.

Sativex, a cannabis-derived medicine which can be sprayed under the tongue, has been available in Canada since 2001. In March 2003, GW Pharmaceuticals submitted a product licence application for Sativex to the UK Medicines and Healthcare Products Regulatory Agency (MHRA).

But despite evidence in small-scale clinical trials that the cannabis derivative THC relieves pain, no licence has been forthcoming. A three-year trial to test whether cannabis derivatives slow the progress of MS as well as alleviating symptoms is just getting under way.

The Home Office announced last

November that the drug could be imported and prescribed by doctors on a 'named patient' basis while still unlicensed but few patients who have asked for it have been able to get it, according to a survey by *Disability Now*.

A cannabis-using MS sufferer who asked not to be named said her request to be prescribed Sativex had been turned down. 'I find it inconceivable that the CPS sees these prosecutions as in the public interest when there is still no legal way for the people who are helped by cannabis to obtain and use it,' she added.

The British Medical Association said in a 1997 report: 'While research is under way the police, the courts and prosecuting authorities should be aware of the medicinal reasons for the unlawful use of cannabis by those suffering from certain medical conditions for whom other drugs have proved ineffective.'

But the Crown Prosecution Service has continued to prosecute both users and suppliers of cannabis for medicinal purposes. Some have been convicted. But others were found not guilty after successfully raising the defence of 'necessity', which allows an illegal act to avert a greater harm – in their cases, severe pain.

Those acquitted included a man with spinal injuries who set up a medical marijuana cooperative, and a doctor who supplied her daughter, whose illness was not specified.

But the appeal court closed off the defence of necessity last year, ruling in six test cases that it did not apply to the use of cannabis to relieve chronic pain.

*17 July 2006*
© *Guardian Newspapers Limited 2006*

# UK 'too soft on cannabis dangers'

New strains of highly potent cannabis are as dangerous as heroin and cocaine and the drug can no longer be dismissed as 'soft and relatively harmless', the United Nations said yesterday.

In an implied criticism of Britain's decision to downgrade cannabis, Antonio Maria Costa, the head of the UN Office on Drugs and Crime, said that countries got the 'drug problem they deserved' if they maintained inadequate policies.

> **New strains of highly potent cannabis are as dangerous as heroin and cocaine and the drug can no longer be dismissed as 'soft and relatively harmless'**

His comments indicated deep unhappiness with the Government's decision to reclassify cannabis from a Class B drug to Class C. Heroin and cocaine are Class A substances, attracting the toughest penalties for possession and trafficking.

'Policy reversals leave young people confused as to just how dangerous cannabis is,' said Mr Costa, introducing the Vienna-based organisation's annual report.

'With cannabis-related health damage increasing, it is fundamentally wrong for countries to make cannabis control dependent on which party is in government. The cannabis pandemic, like other challenges to public health, requires consensus, a consistent commitment across the political spectrum and by society at large.'

Mr Costa said that cannabis was now 'considerably more potent' than a few decades ago. It was 'a mistake' to dismiss it as a soft drug.

**By Philip Johnston, Home Affairs Editor**

'Today the harmful characteristics of cannabis are no longer that different from those of other plant-based drugs such as cocaine and heroin,' he said.

The UN report estimates that 160 million people use the drug worldwide, with a growing market for stronger strains – known as skunk, among other names – which are far stronger than when most of today's policy-makers were young.

The study claimed that a 'significant' number of cannabis users had experienced panic attacks, paranoia and 'psychotic symptoms' during cannabis intoxication – dangers heightened by the growing availability of stronger varieties.

It said: 'Despite early claims to the contrary, cannabis dependence is a reality. Many people who use cannabis find it difficult to stop, even when it interferes with other aspects of their lives, and more than a million people from all over the world enter treatment for cannabis dependence each year.

'Research indicates that younger users, whose brains are still developing, may be especially vulnerable to the negative effects of cannabis. Despite its normalisation in some countries and its occasional celebration in popular culture, it should be noted that cannabis is a powerful drug that has recently become more powerful in many parts of the world.'

Britain downgraded cannabis two years ago in an effort to free police resources to concentrate on 'serious' drugs, such as crack and heroin. A review of that decision in January this year retained the current classification.

David Davis, the shadow home secretary, said the UN report indicated that 'the Government's seriously confused course of action on cannabis has led to chaos and confusion'.

The Home Office emphasised that cannabis remained illegal even if its classification had been lowered. It claimed that its use had declined among young people.

> New strains of cannabis are as dangerous as heroin says UN

A spokesman said: 'It is harmful and illegal and no one should take it.'

The report also expressed concern about growing cocaine use, particularly in western Europe, where demand was reaching 'alarming levels'.

> **'It is harmful and illegal and no one should take it'**

'I urge European Union governments not to ignore this peril,' Mr Costa said. 'Too many professional, educated Europeans use cocaine, often denying their addiction, and drug abuse by celebrities is often presented uncritically by the media leaving young people confused and vulnerable.'

A report from the European Union's Monitoring Centre for Drugs and Drug Addiction said that drug deaths in Europe were at their highest ever.

*27 June 2006*

© *Telegraph Group Limited 2006*

# YouGov drugs survey results

**Thinking about soft drugs such as cannabis, which ONE of the following statements comes closest to your view?**

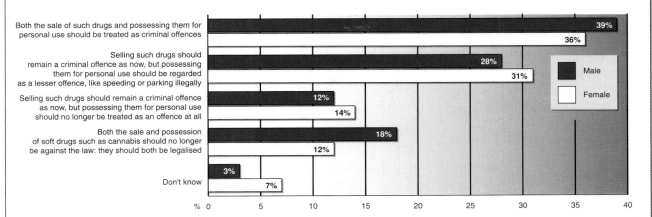

Both the sale of such drugs and possessing them for personal use should be treated as criminal offences — Male 39%, Female 36%

Selling such drugs should remain a criminal offence as now, but possessing them for personal use should be regarded as a lesser offence, like speeding or parking illegally — Male 28%, Female 31%

Selling such drugs should remain a criminal offence as now, but possessing them for personal use should no longer be treated as an offence at all — Male 12%, Female 14%

Both the sale and possession of soft drugs such as cannabis should no longer be against the law: they should both be legalised — Male 18%, Female 12%

Don't know — Male 3%, Female 7%

**As you probably know, different illegal drugs are classified from A to C, roughly according to how much harm they cause to individuals and society. If you think you know, please indicate how each of the following drugs is currently classified, whether A, B or C – cannabis**

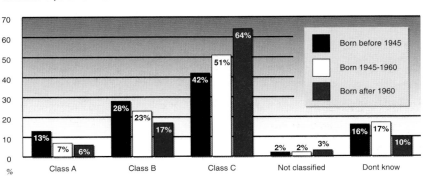

| | Class A | Class B | Class C | Not classified | Dont know |
|---|---|---|---|---|---|
| Born before 1945 | 13% | 28% | 42% | 2% | 16% |
| Born 1945-1960 | 7% | 23% | 51% | 2% | 17% |
| Born after 1960 | 6% | 17% | 64% | 3% | 10% |

**Please indicate, from what you know, how addictive each of these substances are likely to be, in the sense that people become heavily dependent on them either physically or psychologically.**

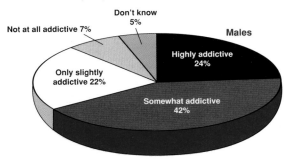

**Males**
- Highly addictive 24%
- Somewhat addictive 42%
- Only slightly addictive 22%
- Not at all addictive 7%
- Don't know 5%

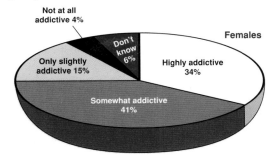

**Females**
- Highly addictive 34%
- Somewhat addictive 41%
- Only slightly addictive 15%
- Not at all addictive 4%
- Don't know 6%

**It is sometimes said that people 'move on' from using soft drugs to using hard ones. From what you know, which ONE of the following statements comes closest to the truth?**

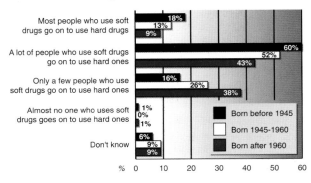

| | Born before 1945 | Born 1945-1960 | Born after 1960 |
|---|---|---|---|
| Most people who use soft drugs go on to use hard drugs | 18% | 13% | 9% |
| A lot of people who use soft drugs go on to use hard ones | 60% | 52% | 43% |
| Only a few people who use soft drugs go on to use hard ones | 16% | 26% | 38% |
| Almost no one who uses soft drugs goes on to use hard ones | 1% | 0% | 1% |
| Don't know | 6% | 9% | 9% |

**Please indicate, from what you know, the amounts of harm that cannabis is likely to cause to individuals and their families and friends.**

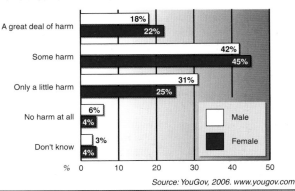

| | Male | Female |
|---|---|---|
| A great deal of harm | 18% | 22% |
| Some harm | 42% | 45% |
| Only a little harm | 31% | 25% |
| No harm at all | 6% | 4% |
| Don't know | 3% | 4% |

*Source: YouGov, 2006. www.yougov.com*

# KEY FACTS

- Cost varies widely around the country. Grass is usually more expensive than resin (hash). (page 1)

- There is a minimal risk of physical dependence on cannabis. Psychological dependency occurs in about 10% of users. (page 2)

- Cannabis is one of the world's most commonly used leisure drugs. It is estimated that at least one person in ten in the UK has used it. (page 3)

- Cannabis is considered by many to have beneficial medicinal applications as an appetite stimulant, muscle relaxant, anxiety-reducing drug and analgesic. (page 4)

- Smoking is by far the most common method of taking cannabis. Like tobacco, cannabis smoke contains toxins that are known to be hazardous to the respiratory system. (page 5)

- 9.7% of 16- to 59-year-olds reported having used cannabis in the last year. In total over 9 million people in the 16- 59 age group have used it at least once with just over 3 million having used it in the last year. (page 6)

- The trend in UK public opinion, particularly among under-35s, is towards support for decriminalisation of cannabis use (but not for other illegal drugs) though not necessarily full-scale legalisation. (page 7)

- Conventional drug treatment services in the UK sometimes regard cannabis use as a low priority unless there is evidence of an underlying mental health problem. (page 10)

- *Cannabis sativa* and *cannabis indica* are members of the nettle family that have grown wild throughout the world for centuries. Both plants have been used for a variety of purposes including hemp to make rope and textiles, as a medical herb and as the popular recreational drug. (page 13)

- A new Dutch study published in the February issue of the *British Journal of Psychiatry* found that cannabis use is associated with 'externalising' problems (delinquent and aggressive behaviour), but not with 'internalising' problems (withdrawn behaviour and depression). (page 16)

- There is still a wide-scale debate raging in the medical community over whether there is any link between lung cancer and smoking cannabis. No overwhelming proof of this link has been discovered and a general conclusion has yet to be reached. (page 17)

- Smoking a joint a couple of nights a week may take 21-28 days to clear the system. Heavy cannabis use may be detected in the system up to 42-56 days later. (page 20)

- Cannabis is by far the most commonly used illegal substance in Europe. Recent population surveys indicate that between 3% and 31% of adults (aged 15 to 64 years) have tried the substance at least once (lifetime use). (page 21)

- Global production of cannabis is estimated at 45,000 metric tons. (page 23)

- 29,520kg of cannabis herb were seized in the UK in 2004, making it the 13th highest-ranking country. (page 25)

- Almost half (48%) of cannabis possession cases received a police caution, compared with less than a quarter (23%) of production cases. (page 31)

- Drug users caught in possession of enough cannabis for just 10 joints could be classified as dealers and face up to 14 years in jail under proposals being considered in Whitehall. (page 32)

- An estimated 4 per cent of the world's adult population consumes cannabis each year, more than all the other illicit drugs combined. In some countries, more than half of the young people polled have tried it. (page 32)

- When users smoke cannabis the THC is absorbed into the blood stream, which takes it from the lungs to the heart and then the brain. THC mimics the actions of receptors in the brain called neurotransmitters and interferes with normal functions. It stimulates brain receptors in the frontal cortex, enabling users to experience heightened senses and a general feeling of relaxation. (page 34)

- Prosecutors are taking a firm line on the supply of cannabis for pain relief to people with chronically painful conditions such as multiple sclerosis, despite the downgrading of the drug from class B to class C. (page 37)

- New strains of highly potent cannabis are as dangerous as heroin and cocaine and the drug can no longer be dismissed as 'soft and relatively harmless', the United Nations has said. (page 38)

- 18% of men surveyed believed both the sale and posession of cannabis should be legal. (page 39)

# GLOSSARY

## Cannabis

Also called marijuana. Slang names include black, dope, draw, ganja, grass, hash, pot, puff, reefer, resin, skunk, spliff, wacky backy and weed. Cannabis is a naturally occuring drug made from parts of the cannabis plant, commonly called hemp. It's a mild hallucinogen and often gives sedative-like effects that make some people feel chilled out ('stoned' or 'high') and others feel sick. It is the most widely used illegal drug in Britain, and can be eaten, inhaled using a bong, or smoked, usually mixed with tobacco, in a pipe or cannabis cigarette (known as a spliff or joint).

## Cannabis oil

A treacle-like liquid, refined from cannabis resin or, less frequently, from the plant itself.

## Cannabis psychosis

There is some evidence that cannabis can result in a short-lived psychotic disorder which subsides fairly quickly once the sufferer stops cannabis use. However, it is quite rare: research in Denmark found only 100 new cases per year.

## Gateway theory

Also called the escalation hypothesis. This refers to the idea that cannabis users are more likely to progress to harder drugs such as heroin. This theory is hotly debated: it is true that most people who use heroin have previously used cannabis, but only a small proportion of those who try cannabis then go on to use heroin.

## Grass (weed)

The dried leaves of the cannabis plant.

## Medicinal cannabis

There is some evidence that cannabis use alleviates the painful symptoms of some diseases, such as Multiple Sclerosis. Many argue that cannabis-based medicines such as Sativex (currently licensed in Canada but not the UK) should be legalised for sufferers of these illnesses.

## Mental health

There is growing evidence that people with mental illnesses such as schizophrenia and depression are more likely to use or have used cannabis for long periods of time in the past. Some claim that cannabis is the cause of these mental health problems, but this has not yet been conclusively proven.

## The 'munchies'

A term sometimes used to describe the hunger pangs which are often experienced while using cannabis.

## Reclassification

Cannabis was reclassified in 2004 from a class B to a class C drug. It is still illegal, and the maximum sentence for possession is two years in prison and an unlimited fine. The maximum penalty for supplying is 14 years in prison and an unlimited fine.

## Resin (hash)

A black-brown lump made from the resin of the cannabis plant.

## Sinsemilla

A bud grown in the absence of male cannabis plants which has no seeds.

## Skunk

Technically, this is a stronger smelling, high-strength herbal cannabis. However, often the labelling of cannabis has no bearing on its actual content: many varieties sold as skunk are no more than mass-produced standard cannabis variants.

## THC

An abbreviation of delta-9-tetrahydrocannabinol. This is the main psychoactive ingredient in cannabis and leads to the feeling of being 'stoned'. Cannabis is one of the most easily detectable drugs when carrying out drugs tests, as this ingredient can take weeks to clear from the body.

# INDEX

# Additional Resources

### Other Issues titles

If you are interested in researching further some of the issues raised in *The Cannabis Issue*, you may like to read the following titles in the **Issues** series:

⇨ Vol. 123 *Young People and Health* (ISBN 978 1 86168 362 5)
⇨ Vol. 114 *Drug Abuse* (ISBN 978 1 86168 347 2)
⇨ Vol. 93 *Binge Drinking* (ISBN 978 1 86168 301 4)
⇨ Vol. 86 *Smoking and your Health* (ISBN 978 1 86168 287 1)
⇨ Vol. 84 *Mental Wellbeing* (ISBN 978 1 86168 279 6)

For more information about these titles, visit our website at www.independence.co.uk/publicationslist

### Useful organisations

You may find the websites of the following organisations useful for further research:

⇨ Drugscope: www.drugscope.org.uk
⇨ FRANK: www.talktofrank.com
⇨ HIT: www.knowcannabis.org.uk
⇨ Release: www.release.org.uk
⇨ SHEU: www.sheu.org.uk

# ACKNOWLEDGEMENTS

The publisher is grateful for permission to reproduce the following material.

While every care has been taken to trace and acknowledge copyright, the publisher tenders its apology for any accidental infringement or where copyright has proved untraceable. The publisher would be pleased to come to a suitable arrangement in any such case with the rightful owner.

## Chapter One: Cannabis Issues

Cannabis, © FRANK, Cannabis – in depth, © Release, Cannabis facts, © DrugScope, Cannabis information, © HIT, Does cannabis lead to taking other drugs?, © DrugScope, Reducing, or stopping, cannabis use, © Release, Drug misuse, © Crown copyright is reproduced with the permission of Her Majesty's Stationery Office, Vulnerability to hard drugs, © Neuropsychopharmacology, Public relaxed on use of cannabis, © Telegraph Group Limited 2006, Cannabis and mental health, © Royal College of Psychiatrists, Cannabis and problem behaviour, © Royal College of Psychiatrists, Cannabis and lung cancer, © TheSite.org, A smoking gun?, © British Lung Foundation, Drug testing at work, © TheSite. org, The state of the cannabis problem in Europe, © EMCDDA, The cannabis market – production, © UNODC.

## Chapter Two: Cannabis and the Law

Drug laws and licensing, © Crown copyright is reproduced with the permission of Her Majesty's Stationery Office, Kate's story, © FRANK, Common misconceptions about reclassification, © UKCIA, Why drug laws damage cannabis users' health, © Lifeline, Cannabis users with just 10 joints face 14 years' jail, © Telegraph Group Limited 2006, Cannabis: why we should care, © UNODC, Cannabis: the science, © TheSite.org, Your rights on arrest, © Release, Cannabis and cannabis extracts, © Multiple Sclerosis Society, Medicinal cannabis and the law, © Guardian Newspapers Ltd 2006, UK 'too soft on cannabis dangers', © Telegraph Group Ltd 2006.

## Photographs and illustrations:

Pages 3, 20: Bev Aisbett; pages 8, 16, 22: Simon Kneebone; pages 10, 19, 35: Don Hatcher; pages 17, 18, 27: Angelo Madrid.

And with thanks to the team: Mary Chapman, Sandra Dennis and Jan Haskell.

Lisa Firth
Cambridge
January, 2007